History of American Naval Dry Docks

A Key Ingredient to a Maritime Power

Richard D. Hepburn, P.E.
Captain, U.S. Navy (Retired)

Noesis, Inc.
4100 North Fairfax Drive
Suite 800
Arlington, Virginia 22203-1663
(703) 741-0300
http://www.noesis-inc.com

Library of Congress Cataloging-in-Publication Data

Hepburn, Richard D.
  History of American Naval Dry Docks
  ISBN 0-9742091-0-4
  1. History – United States
  I. Hepburn, Richard D. 1954-   History.

Library of Congress Registration Number Pending

©2003 by Noesis, Inc.

All rights reserved. No part of this book may be reproduced in any form or by any means, without permissions from the publisher.

Printed in the United States of America.

ISBN 0-9742091-0-4

TX 5-747-091

Noesis, Inc.
4100 North Fairfax Drive
Suite 800
Arlington, Virginia   22203-1663
(703) 741-0300

On the world wide web at www.noesis-inc.com.

Table of Contents

Author i
Acknowledgments iii
Foreword v
Introduction vii
Chapter 1 — The World's First Dry Docks 1
Chapter 2 — American Shipyards Emerge 3
Chapter 3 — The Birth of the United States Navy and
            United States Naval Shipyards 5
Chapter 4 — A War and a New Commitment for a Navy
            and New Facilities 11
Chapter 5 — A New Dry Dock at the New York Navy
            Yard – Largest in the World 25
Chapter 6 — More Dry Docks Emerge and Dry Docks
            on the West Coast Emerge 35
Chapter 7 — Naval Repair Facility Expansion Plans
            Continued on the East Coast 45
Chapter 8 — The Salvaging of the *MERRIMACK* in
            the Norfolk (Gosport) Navy Yard Dry Dock 53
Chapter 9 — Post War Pause in the East, but
            Continued Expansion in the West 59
Chapter 10 — Post Civil War Doldrums End and Iron
             Hulls Mean More Drydockings 65
Chapter 11 — The Battleship Age and a New Global View 71
Chapter 12 — Global Reach and the Need for a
             Forward Deployed Floating Dry Dock 85
Chapter 13 — Graving Docks on the West Coast and Hawaii
             Become the Priority 89
Chapter 14 — Panama Canal Completes,
             World War I Starts and
             Dry Dock Construction Surges 95
Chapter 15 — Preparations for Another War 109
Chapter 16 — World War II Begins 119

Chapter 17 — On the Road to Recovery and
Ultimate Victory 125

Chapter 18 — Floating Dry Docks During World
War II and Beyond 133

Chapter 19 — Post World War II High Water Mark for
U.S. Navy Graving Docks 143

Chapter 20 — Other U.S. Navy Ship Drydocking Facilities 149

Chapter 21 — New Innovations in Ship Transport
and Repair 155

Chapter 22 — A 21ST Century Need Lives on for
This Age Old Process 161

Chapter 23 — Conclusion — A Maritime Nation
Needs to Remain Aware of Her Required
Maritme Capacity 167

References E-1

List of Figures F-1

List of Tables T-1

Index I-1

Author

Richard Daniel Hepburn was born in Glendale, California, in 1954 to David and Jacqueline Hepburn. He graduated from the United States Naval Academy in 1976 with a Bachelor of Science degree in Ocean Engineering and received his commission in the U.S. Navy. He earned a Master of Science degree from the Massachusetts Institute of Technology in Naval Architecture and Marine Engineering in 1988. He also earned a Naval Engineer degree from MIT in 1988. His tours at sea included serving as Main Propulsion Assistant and Damage Control Assistant on the *USS MEYERKORD (FF 1058)* and Repair Officer on the *USS PUGET SOUND (AD 38)*. Rick became an Engineering Duty Officer in 1980. Ashore, he served as a Navy officer recruiter at Navy Recruiting District Los Angeles; Ship Superintendent, Docking Officer, and Production Engineer at Long Beach Naval Shipyard; Officer in Charge of the Resident Supervisor of Shipbuilding Office in Savannah, Georgia; Force Engineer and Surface Combatant Type Desk Coordinator for the Commander Naval Surface Force, U.S. Atlantic Fleet; Deputy Director, Power Systems Group and Director, Surface Ship Design and System Engineering Group, Naval Sea Systems Command and Commanding Officer, Supervisor of Shipbuilding, Conversion, and Repair, United States Navy, Bath, Maine. Rick also served as the Docking Officer for the heavy lift of four mine countermeasure ships to and from the Arabian Gulf during Operation Desert Shield and Storm. He published four technical papers with the American Society of Naval Engineers and the Society of Naval Architects and Marine Engineers. He is a registered Professional Engineer in the States of Virginia and Georgia. He was twice elected to the national Council of the American Society of Naval Engineers and is now serving as Vice President of that Society. He is also a graduate of the Advanced Program Managers Course at the Defense Systems Management College. Rick retired from the Navy as a Captain in October 2001 and is currently the Senior Research and Development Coordinator and Project Engineer for Noesis, Inc. located in Arlington, Virginia. While at Noesis Inc., he has written and taught an extensive course on drydocking for the Naval Sea System Command. Rick and his wife Debby reside in Manassas, Virginia. They have three children: Scott, Samantha, and Eric.

Acknowledgments

Without the love, counsel, patience and encouragement of my wife Debby, this book would not have been possible. She kept me on the right track at the many switching stations along the way. She kept me going even when it was not convenient for her. Debby is and forever will be my true love, friend, inspiration and guiding light. She kept the faith and instilled that faith in me. Debby was also my toughest reviewer and profoundly improved this work.

I want to express my deepest appreciation to Phil Sims of the Surface Ship Design Group Naval Sea Systems Command, whose research and sincere interest made this project all the more complete. His technical advice and analysis contributed heavily to the final product. I want to thank Rick Weiser, also of the Naval Sea Systems Command, who I have worked with for over 18 years in world of U.S. Navy drydocking. Dr. David F. Winkler of the Naval Historical Foundation encouraged me to publish this book and spent considerable time reviewing, editing, and providing expert insight and valuable suggestions greatly improving the historical and reading quality of this book.

I greatly appreciate Mr. Rich Martin, President of Noesis Inc., for giving me the opportunity to complete this work and having Noesis Inc. publish it as an historical record. I would also like to thank the sincere interest, professionalism and thoroughness offered by my editor and co-worker, Susan Ecker. Her attention to detail was essential and her enthusiasm was a catalyst that made this work a book. Dr. Terrence Ponick also provided an outstanding professional review.

Finally, and most importantly my Pastor, Edwin Elliott, of the Reformed Presbyterian Church of Manassas, was extremely instrumental in the production of this work. His providential insight and motivation, along with his extensive experience in publishing, provided me the path for success.

Foreword

Writing in the November 1989 issue of *Morskoy Sbornik*, First Deputy Commander in Chief of the Soviet Navy, Vice Admiral Igor V. Kasatonov shared observations of his recent port call at the U.S. Navy Base at Norfolk, Virginia. "Ships there only tie up at piers. The Americans say: "roadsteads eat ships." I think professionals will understand. Standing in a harbor, the ship works on herself—motors suffer wear; fuel is consumed. At Norfolk even the carriers tie up at a pier, linked up to all life-support systems. Our economic planners prefer to economize on the construction of large piers, except that this economizing costs hundreds of thousands in losses."

Over a decade later, most of the once mighty Soviet Navy is laid up rusting within inlets along the Barents Sea, Sea of Japan, and other coastal areas. Part of the explanation for this naval implosion was the lack of investment in infrastructure to accompany the billions of rubles spent on seagoing weapon platforms. The United States, in contrast, had built up a naval shore infrastructure over two centuries that allowed for the maintenance and modernization of its fleet.

Captain Rick Hepburn, a retired Engineering Duty Officer, worked within that naval shore infrastructure for over two decades. A 1976 graduate of the United States Naval Academy, he spent a tour at sea on a frigate, earning his Surface Warfare Officer pin. During a tour in recruiting, he was exposed to the Navy's small but highly professional Engineering Duty Officer (ED) community and the world of shipyards and dry docks. What impressed him was the tremendous amount of responsibility bestowed on a relative junior Engineering Duty Officer in moving ships in and out of a dry dock within two years of his being accepted into the community.

In various tours as an ED, Captain Hepburn is credited with docking or undocking Navy ships or other craft 117 times. He performed the bulk of these evolutions during his first tour as docking officer at Long Beach Naval Shipyard, including the drydocking of the battleship *Missouri* (BB 63). Having responsibility for bringing ships out of water to enable work to be accomplished on their hulls, Captain Hepburn gained an appreciation and interest for these enormous structures.

Indeed, his Masters and Naval Engineers Thesis at the Massachusetts Institute of Technology titled "Nonlinear Three Degree of Freedom Submarine Drydock Blocking Systems" focused on what could happen to ships in graving docks during earthquakes. Recommendations he made to improve the structural integrity of these structures were actually adopted by the Royal Navy.

With an interest in these structures spurred by two decades of hands-on work and research, Captain Hepburn has performed an admirable job of telling the story of dry docks, starting with the first graving dock built in the 1830s at Gosport to the building spurts to support the new steel navy and the "two-ocean" navy that triumphed in World War II, and finally to modern means of lifting ships out of water that are mostly maintained today in the private sector.

In telling the story of U.S. Navy dry docks, Captain Hepburn is also telling a history of the United States Navy through a unique perspective, that maritime power is more than ships. In addition to providing a chronological overview of dry docks, Captain Hepburn has accumulated statistics and facts that make this an important reference work. His collection and selection of blueprints, illustrations, and photography also help to make this book a page turner.

The book concludes with an overview of recent innovations that have led to new ways of lifting ships out of water. Captain Hepburn also notes the loss of numerous shipyards and dry docks to the Base Realignment and Closure (BRAC) process. While understanding the need to consolidate facilities, Captain Hepburn warns that additional infrastructure cuts come at the nation's peril. With that in mind, *History of American Naval Dry Docks* is the type of book that needs to grace the book shelves of the current Navy leaders as well as naval historians.

David F. Winkler, Ph.D.
Naval Historical Foundation

Introduction

The United States of America is and always has been a maritime nation. It is so by necessity as it is surrounded by two oceans and virtually relies almost exclusively on surface shipment of heavy materials and goods via the ocean waters to export and import products overseas. The oceans have also been a safety net, separating the country from the close proximity of war. However, to engage in international trade, to protect the sovereignty of her own shores, and to prevent overseas wars from affecting life and liberty in the United States it was necessary to create a Navy early on that could traverse the seven seas and carry a credible threat with it.

The first three Presidents of the United States, Washington, Adams, and Jefferson, learned early that a strong Navy was necessary to protect the merchant trade and that a coastal defense alone was not adequate. Therefore, at the close of the 18th and the beginning of the 19th century, the Navy emerged as an entity constructing frigate size (44-gun) warships and establishing six United States Navy Yards.

As foreign navies brought their large ships-of-the-line to the shores of the United States and indeed even attacked the Capital of the United States at Washington D.C. in 1814, Congress quickly decided that larger United States warships were also needed. However, larger warships required associated larger ship repair facilities that would allow underwater hull cleaning and repair.

The construction of relatively low capacity marine railways quickly shifted to construction of high capacity dry docks dug out of the ground (called graving docks). These "stone docks" which were constructed of granite stone were large enough to accommodate the drydocking of 74-gun ships-of-the-line. The construction of these dry docks was followed by the construction of floating dry docks which were also relatively high capacity. These floating dry docks were portable and allowed ship repair to expand to the fast growing West Coast of the United States.

As the warship size increased and the shift from wood to steel occurred due to international pressures and three wars (Civil, Spanish, and World War I), so did the requirement for increased dry dock size and capacity. Thus, an ever-expanding compliment of graving docks, floating docks and marine railways emerged, especially during World War II and continuing until the late 1900s.

New methods of drydocking ships emerged in the late 20th Century although conceived in the previous century. These exotic methods were primarily commercially owned, and included heavy lift ships, vertical lifts, and new computer controlled floating dry docks. The U.S. Navy contracted for the use of these drydocking facilities rather than invest in sole ownership. A recent example of this was the heavy lift of the *USS COLE (DDG 67)* from the Gulf of Aden in the Middle East to Pascagoula, Mississippi October to December 2000 on the Norwegian heavy lift ship *M/V BLUE MARLIN*. With the dawn of the new century and millennium, the private sector's new warship construction shipyards have been reduced to six with two corporations owning these six yards. These corporations, Northrop Grumman Ship Systems and General Dynamics are modernizing their facilities to include new or upgraded cranes and floating dry docks to accommodate yet another new class of ship, the DDX, while reducing the number of production man-hours to produce these highly complex ships using "lean manufacturing" techniques.

With the end of the Vietnam War and the Cold War, the United States Navy again substantially reduced its number of warships as happened after the Revolutionary, Civil, and World Wars. This time, however, the era of United States Navy-owned dry dock construction ended, and for the first time in United States history the Navy substantially reduced the number of its government-owned dry docks.

With the massive cost of graving dock construction or activation, the significant environmental impacts and requirements, the movement toward commercialization of government facilities, the availability of commercially owned dry docks, and the increased scarcity of waterfront property, the United States Navy will never again own and operate over 62 graving docks and 106 floating dry docks. U.S. Navy dry dock facility ownership and operation has indeed peaked and ebbed. While the need could arise again for a large number of government owned dry docks, it is doubtful that this will occur any time soon with the increasing drive to outsourcing and privatization in a world getting more globalized and hopefully more peaceful. The only caution is that this would be a first in United States history.

The need for a sizable Navy was again demonstrated during the war with Iraq early in 2003 when 72 percent of the Navy was deployed while threats from North Korea were simultaneously occurring. Senior Navy leadership is now professing the need for a larger number of surface combatants. Increasing the number of ships will prove easier than increasing the number of shipyards and dry docks required to maintain these ships. Some of the closed Naval shipyards have been abandoned or converted into container ports with the shops bulldozed and the dry docks filled in.

This book tells the story of an epic period of American maritime history: the people, the ideas, the inventions, and the incredible structures they built that helped make the United States of America and the United States Navy what it is today. It is history we need to learn and view with wonder, accented by lessons demonstrating a continued need for ship repair drydocking facilities.

Chapter 1

The World's First Dry Docks

In early American architecture, most concepts originated from British construction. This was the case with dry docks as well. Dry dock construction in Great Britain blossomed with their first naval expansion. The world's first dry dock was ordered constructed by King Henry VII in 1495 at Portsmouth, England. It was designed by Sir Reginald Bray, architect of the Henry VII Chapel at Westminster Abby.

> "... the emergence of an English navy during the reign of Henry VII coincided with the establishment of the first permanent royal dockyard. This was at Portsmouth which, in 1496, received a purpose built dry dock that allowed warships to be drawn out of the water so that their hulls might be repaired and cleaned."[1]

King Charles II created the Royal Navy in 1670 and shortly thereafter ordered the construction of the first stone docks (called graving docks) at Portsmouth, England. The granite stones used in this effort were excavated from English quarries. The large stones formed the walls and floor of the dry docks.[2] These dry docks had to be used in conjunction with changing tide levels. The harbor of Portsmouth is well suited for dry docks as it has favorable tides caused in part by its location in relation to the Isle of White which has two accesses to the sea. The dry docks were designed to take advantage of the tidal height differences. The low tide periods were used for maintenance and the cleaning of the ships' bottoms.

The French, in 1669 at Rochefort, built the first masonry type dry dock. This dry dock was called the 'Vielle-Forme.'[3] About thirty years later, around 1700 a British Royal Navy Captain, while trading in the Baltic, created the World's first floating dry dock.[4] It was actually an old hulk where the beams and deck were removed and a watertight gate was put at one end. This type of dry dock was required due to the lack of sufficient tides in the Baltic Sea. It was actually similar in concept to a graving dock in that it was an enclosed basin which was pumped out once a ship was in place. This type of dock was similar to what was later referred to as a camel floating dock.[5]

By the end of the 1700s, the Royal Navy's Portsmouth Dockyard was in the forefront of the Industrial Revolution. In 1799, the first steam engine was used to pump out these dry docks. In 1801, Sir Samuel Bentham built the world's first caisson for the Royal Dockyards. A caisson is a vessel that can be ballasted with water and sunk into a sill at the dock entrance. This seals the dry dock and allows it to be pumped out rather than having to rely on the tidal range to empty it.[6]

These early dry docks still exist, and are now used to permanently exhibit Admiral Nelson's historic warship *HMS VICTORY* and salvaged portions of King Henry VIII's warship *MARY ROSE*. A similar dry dock was constructed at the Devonport Dockyard in 1693 near Plymouth, England. The dockyard at Devonport is still the largest Naval dockyard in Western Europe. All of these dry docks exist today and some are still used by the Royal Navy.

Chapter 2

American Shipyards Emerge

Shipyards in America started a long time before the Revolutionary War. Europeans populated North America as a result of sea travel by ships. Therefore, the need for ship repair in America was an immediate consequence. As Virginia was the root of English colonization of America; Portsmouth, Virginia was the site of the first shipyard, established by a Scotsman named Andrew Sprowle in 1767 when he purchased a sixteen-acre tract of land from local residents.[7]

Sprowle named his shipyard Gosport and it was located adjacent to Portsmouth, Virginia, across the Elizabeth River from what later became the City of Norfolk. These names were obviously derived from the key British ports of Portsmouth and Gosport located adjacent to each other in Southern England. The British Union Jack was the first flag raised over the Gosport Yard in 1767, and the yard remained under that flag until 1775.[8]

The Gosport Yard became the property of the Commonwealth of Virginia at the outbreak of the Revolutionary War. The Gosport Yard was the largest shipyard in Virginia and heavily contributed to the construction of the Virginia's Navy, the largest in all the colonies. Being the prize that it was, the shipyard was occupied and burned for the first time by the Royal Navy in 1779.[9] Admiral Sir George Collier, Commander of the British fleet which occupied Portsmouth said the following regarding the burning of the Gosport Yard:

> " . . . the marine-yard was the most considerable one in America . . . large and extremely convenient . . . Five thousand loads of fine seasoned oak-knees for shipbuilding, an infinite quantity of plank, masts, cordage, and numbers of beautiful ships of war on the stocks, were at one time in a blaze." [10]

After the end of the American Revolution, interest in any type of Navy waned. There was no immediate desire on the part of the individual states to have a strong central government, Federal taxes, and therefore a Navy. Two years after the end of the War,

Congress sold off the last ship of the Continental Navy. The naval work at the shipyard at Gosport came to a close for the time being.

Another important footnote from the American Revolution relates to one of its heroic veterans and the father of the original engineer of America's first two graving docks. The Revolutionary hero was Colonel Loammi Baldwin, 1740-1807, and his son was Loammi Baldwin II, 1780-1838. Colonel Baldwin of Woburn, Massachusetts was present at the Battle of Lexington which started the Revolution. He also led the 26th Regiment of the Continental Army for General George Washington in the Battle of Trenton on December 26, 1776.[11] His prodigal son, born just 4 years later, assisted in designing the monument at Bunker Hill and is considered the father of American Civil Engineering. Loammi Baldwin II's exploits as the designer of the first and second graving docks for the United States Navy made him a pillar in American Naval history and he is discussed later in this book.

Chapter 3

The Birth of the United States Navy and United States Naval Shipyards

The strong desire for trade on the part of American merchants and the restrictions on trade in the West Indies levied by the British after the Revolution, caused American Merchants to seek out trade in the Mediterranean markets. As trade increased, so did the danger. The Barbary States of North Africa made a habit of preying on merchant ships. With no Navy to protect them, American merchants were appealing targets and quickly fell victim to these pirates. It is interesting that one of the largest threats to merchant shipping in the South China Sea in 2000 was pirates. American merchant ships are still not immune to this threat.

To protect American commerce from Algerian corsairs and to prevent further capture of American merchant sailors, on April 22, 1793, President George Washington recommended to Congress the construction of six frigates. President Washington's administration took a political tack to assure Congressional approval. They selected six different sites for ship construction in six different States. Materials were to be purchased from many states including timber from the southern states of North Carolina, South Carolina, and Georgia.[12] Congress passed the Navy Act or "An Act to Provide a Naval Armament" on March 27, 1794, which approved the purchase of the construction of these six frigates.[13] This act effectively founded the United States Navy.

Even with a newly established desire for a navy, there were no navy yards to build these frigates, so the facilities were leased . The ship construction would be under the supervision of Navy agents and yard clerks. For all intents, this was the origin of the first U.S. Navy Supervisors of Shipbuilding (SUPSHIP). A SUPSHIP office still exists at all major private yards building U.S. Navy ships today, although there are major consolidations of these offices underway at the time this book is being published.

In 1794, the task of construction was huge. Six different shipyards had to be built or reconfigured to build the largest ships ever built by the United States. Skilled craftsman had to be found to fill these six yards, along with competent supervisors and ultimately the officers and crews to man the ships once they were completed.

In 1794, the United States leased, but did not purchase, the Gosport Yard from the Commonwealth of Virginia for the construction of *CHESAPEAKE*. Mr. William Pennock was appointed Navy Agent; Captain Richard Dale, the eventual commanding officer of *CHESAPEAKE*, was appointed Superintendent; and the Mr. Josiah Fox was appointed constructor or master builder.[14]

It was decided that the frigates would be built on building "ways." When construction was complete, the ships would slide down on greased "ways" or tracks and float off the building carriage into the adjacent body of water. The premier naval architect during the Revolution, Joshua Humphreys of Philadelphia, was selected as the naval architect of the frigates. Humphreys came to this job having been tasked by Congress during the Revolution to refit eight merchant vessels as the first ships of the Continental Navy in 1775. His design is still marveled at by the hundreds of visitors who come to visit the *USS CONSTITUTION* in Boston each day. Humphreys was the first naval constructor (1794-1801) and designed the first six frigates for the United States Navy. He personally supervised the construction of *USS UNITED STATES* that launched in 1797.

Construction of these U.S. Navy frigates commenced at Joshua Humphreys' own South Philadelphia shipyard situated at the foot of Federal Street.[15] By no coincidence, the Capitol of the United States at the time was Philadelphia. The *UNITED STATES* launched on May 10, 1797.

The next frigate, *CONSTELLATION* launched at Baltimore, Maryland on September 7, 1797, and *CONSTITUTION* launched next at Boston after some difficulty getting the ship off the ways on October 21, 1797. Three of the six frigates were launched the same year in 1797, only three years since Congress passed the Navy Act. This was an amazing feat by any standard. The

United States Navy would be only too happy to have such a building rate in the year 2003!

Joshua Humphreys first designed the vessels as 44-gun frigates, but it was finally decided to build the last three as 36-gun frigates. This was most likely a cost savings move, much like today's shipbuilding programs when capabilities are reduced to meet budget constraints.

With naval construction in progress, considerable public monies at stake, and the threat of war with France looming, Congress on April 30, 1798 created the Department of the Navy at cabinet rank. Benjamin Stoddard of Maryland became the first Secretary of the Navy.[16] Thus, the creation of the office of the Secretary of Navy was rooted in shipbuilding. Later that year, on December 10, 1798, the keel was laid for the *CHESAPEAKE* at the Gosport Yard in Virginia.

Shipbuilding continued in earnest with the launching of *CONGRESS* at Portsmouth, New Hampshire on August 15, 1799. The Portsmouth Yard was to become a U.S. Navy Yard the following year. On December 2, 1799, *CHESAPEAKE* was launched at the Gosport Yard. Also in 1799, the 36-gun frigate *PHILADELPHIA* (built with private funds and not one of the six original appropriated frigates) was launched from Joshua Humphreys' yard and later presented to the U.S. Navy. The last of the original six frigates completed was the *PRESIDENT* which was launched at New York on April 1, 1800.[17]

With six frigates now in service, the immediate need for Navy owned docking and repair locations became apparent. The private yards were found to be too small, with inadequate dock and warehouse space. The creation of the United States Navy Yards occurred in 1800 when Congress appropriated funds to establish six of them.

I was honored to attend the celebration of the 200th anniversary of Portsmouth Naval Shipyard celebrated on June 10, 2000 and Admiral Frank Lee "Skip" Bowman, USN, Director, Naval Nuclear Propulsion, and Vice Admiral George "Pete" Nanos, USN, Commander Naval Sea Systems Command participated in this historic event, along with the Congressional delegations from the States of Maine and New Hampshire.

An interesting side note: Not quite a year after this celebration, in May 2001, the U.S. Supreme Court decided that the Portsmouth Naval Shipyard was indeed located in the State of Maine and not in New Hampshire. At the time, I was the Supervisor of Shipbuilding in Bath, Maine. I sent an email to the then Commander of Portsmouth Naval Shipyard, Capt Tom Williams, and welcomed him to the State of Maine.

Congress's appropriation in 1800 also included the purchase of Joshua Humphreys' yard and some surrounding land for what would become the Philadelphia Naval Shipyard at a cost of $38,636.[18] In addition, the Federal Government purchased the Gosport Yard from the Commonwealth of Virginia. The deed for 16 acres (Andrew Sprowle's original shipyard property) was signed on 15 June 1801 by James Monroe, then Governor of Virginia, for the sum of $12,000.[19]

The Charlestown Navy Yard at Charlestown, Massachusetts, across the Charles River from Boston, was also one of the six original naval shipyards established in 1800-1801."[20] The others were Portsmouth, New Hampshire; New York (Brooklyn), New York; Philadelphia, Pennsylvania; Gosport (Portsmouth/Norfolk), Virginia; and the Washington Navy Yard, District of Columbia.

Construction of significant facilities at these yards occurred gradually. The following account describes the beginnings of the Federal administration of the Gosport Yard:

> "This Gosport Yard tract was situated in the northeast corner of the present shipyard and erected upon it, prior to 1827, were the following structures: an office, a commandant's house, Marine barracks, brick storehouse which stood near the First Street Gate, a powder magazine, a 'smithery', and two large covered building-ways known as 'ship-houses'." [21]

This build up was short lived as, after the Quasi-War with France (1798-1800), Congress voted on March 3, 1801 to reduce the size of the Navy. President Thomas Jefferson, who took office on March 4, 1801, whole-heartedly agreed. All American ships were sold except the brig *ENTERPRISE* and 13 frigates.[22] Jefferson desired a gunboat navy for coastal defense only. However, this policy also did not survive long as the Pasha of Tripoli declared war on the United States due to insufficient tribute on May 14, 1801. Fortunately, there was still a semblance of a Navy, and on May 20, 1801 the first American squadron was deployed to the Mediterranean Sea.

It is interesting to note that President Jefferson was interested in practical means of maintaining ships. In his annual message to Congress (what is now the "State of the Union Address"), Jefferson discussed the requirement for building a dry dock. But he went beyond that. Jefferson foresaw a means for laying up a number of ships at one time, protected from the weather. What he was visualizing was what would become a land level transfer facility over one hundred and sixty years later. The plan presented under the direction of the President in American State papers (Naval affairs) by B. H. Latrope envisioned a facility that could lay up (moth ball) twelve 44-gun frigates.[23]

Apparently, President Jefferson wanted to preserve his Navy if not use it actively. He personally professed his concerns about the proper preservation of naval vessels, if for no other reason than financial necessity:

> "no cares, no attentions, can preserve vessels from rapid decay which lie in the water exposed to the sun. This decay requires extensive and constant repairs, and will consume, if continued, a great portion of the money destined for naval purposes."[24]

Chapter 4

A War and a New Commitment for a Navy and New Facilities

It took the War of 1812 to clearly demonstrate the need for a strong Navy. In this war, the nation's capitol, Washington D.C., was itself attacked and burned. During this disaster on August 24 and 25, 1814, the frigates *BOSTON*, *GENERAL GREEN*, and *NEW YORK* and two ships under construction, the frigate *COLUMBIA* and the sloop *ARGUS (II)*, were all destroyed to prevent their capture by the British at the Washington Navy Yard.[25]

This close call brought a different response by Congress after the War of 1812 compared to earlier and later wars. Congress now saw the immediate need for a larger Navy, and on April 29, 1816, approved eight million dollars for the construction of nine 74-gun ships of the line and twelve frigates of 44 guns.

At the Portsmouth Navy Yard, in 1814, one of the 74-gun ships-of-the-line, was constructed and christened the *USS WASHINGTON*, the first naval vessel named after our first president. The shipyard constructed 13 more ships for the United States Navy prior to the Civil War, earning its nickname, "Cradle of American Shipbuilding."[26]

At the Gosport Navy Yard, the construction of the 74-gun ships-of-the-line brought about immediate change:

> "Expansion and improvement changed the Navy Yard after the War of 1812 and the period was marked by a number of events, outstanding in their day. The keel of the ship-of-the-line *DELAWARE*, the first of its type ever to be built here, was laid in the summer of 1817, and it was launched October 21, 1820, with due ceremony attended by the local populace. ..."[27]

The presence of these enormous warships were coincident with the invention of steam propulsion. In 1815, the age of steam powered ships began for the United States Navy. At the New York Navy

Yard, Robert Fulton's steam frigate, *Fulton*, launched.[28] With larger and heavier ships in the Navy, more advanced repair facilities were required.

In 1822, Commodore John Rodgers designed and built the first marine railway in the United States at the Washington Navy Yard, Washington, DC.[29] Commodore Rogers was the President of the Navy Board at the time. In a communication dated December 23, 1822, he submitted a plan for this marine railway. Commodore Rogers' desire was:

> "to place them [ships] under cover, protected from the sun, rain, etc., without incurring the least risk; and universal experience proves that a vessel placed in such a situation, may be preserved almost any length of time."[30]

The Secretary of the Navy, the Honorable Smith Thompson, agreed with Commodore Rogers and stated:

> "I have carefully examined these papers and fully accord with the President of the Navy Board, as to the utility, and great importance of the inclined plane and dock, for the purpose mentioned in the specifications, and I recommend the same to your favorable consideration."[31]

This railway was operated using manpower to haul the ships out of the water for hull repairs and preservation. The first ship to use this marine railway was the frigate *USS POTOMAC*. The President and members of Congress attended the event. It took 140 men to haul the ship out of the water using this railway.[32]

The President of the United States at the time was James Monroe. He had just pressured Spain into ceding Florida to the United States in 1819. Spain's American colonies rebelled and European powers threatened to intervene. This led to the Monroe Doctrine that President Monroe outlined during his annual address to Congress in 1823.[33] President Monroe announced that:

> "the U.S. would regard interference in American affairs as an unfriendly act and the western hemisphere was closed to further European colonization. The latter statement [was also] designed to check Russian expansion on the Pacific coast."[34]

In addition, President Monroe constructed a chain of coastal fortifications to prevent future invasions.[35] His strong message of no foreign intervention was coupled with an increase in national defenses.

In 1823, a permanent marine railway and large covered shiphouse was built at the Washington Navy Yard.[36] Figure (1) is an illustration of this facility at that time.

Figure 1 - Drawing of the first marine railway in the United States at the Washington Navy Yard designed in 1822 by Commodore John Rodgers. (Government Printing Office)

The marine railway alone was not adequate to take care of the maintenance required of the new ships-of-the-line. Congress passed "An Act for the Gradual Improvement of the Navy of the United States," on March 3, 1827.[37] This resulted in the design and construction of two stone (graving) docks similar to the dry docks in Portsmouth and Devonport Dock Yards in Britain. One stone dry dock was to be constructed at the Charlestown Navy Yard near Boston, Massachusetts and the other at the Gosport Navy Yard at Norfolk, Virginia.

The dry docks at Charlestown and Gosport Navy Yards were both designed and the construction supervised by an engineer named Loammi Baldwin II. Baldwin was the son of a famous American Revolutionary War Veteran, Colonel Loammi Baldwin, of Woburn, Massachusetts.[38] Colonel Baldwin was himself an accomplished scientist and author, and obviously had a profound influence on his son.

Loammi Baldwin II was born in 1780, three years after his father left the Continental Army due to ill health. As was mentioned earlier, Colonel Baldwin had commanded a company from Woburn under General Washington during the Battle of Trenton on December 26, 1776. Colonel Baldwin was extensively involved in the design of the Middlesex Canal in Massachusetts completed in 1803. He also developed what later became known as the Baldwin Apple.[39]

With this innovative family environment as background, Loammi Baldwin II soon began his own illustrious engineering career. He actually started out with a law degree from Harvard in 1800. He traveled to Europe in 1807 and gained an appreciation and affection for the World's civil engineering achievements.

Upon Baldwin's return to New England, he became involved in military construction as result of the ongoing War of 1812 with Britain. As a resident of Charlestown, Massachusetts in 1814, Baldwin designed and supervised fortifications at Fort Strong in Boston Harbor.

After the War, Baldwin continued his civil engineering work and was placed in charge of public improvements for the City of Boston. This included the extension of Beacon Street and the beginnings of the project that created what is now the Back Bay.

During this period, Baldwin demonstrated his mechanical engineering ability by designing the first steam-powered fire pump engine used at Groton, Connecticut. This skill became useful later on in the design of dry dock pumping systems.

Baldwin again traveled to Europe in 1824 and observed the functioning dry docks in England and Antwerp.[40] He gained first hand knowledge of the European's enormous engineering achievements in the field of graving dock design and construction. When he returned home, he continued to pursue civil projects and honored Revolutionary War Veterans like his father by assisting in the design and erection of the Bunker Hill Monument.

Upon Baldwin's commission from the United States Navy to construct the first two graving docks in the United States, he quickly decided to make the two designs identical. Both dry docks were built from the same set of plans, and were constructed of huge granite blocks on wooden piles. The granite came from the same quarry at Quincy, Massachusetts. The blocks for the Norfolk dry dock were loaded aboard ships for the trip south.

Work started in June 1827, on the Boston dry dock at the Charlestown Navy Yard. Baldwin appointed Alexander Parris, who worked with him on the Bunker Hill Monument, to be his principal assistant for the construction at Charlestown. Similarly, he appointed Captain William P.S. Sanger to be his principal assistant for the construction at Norfolk.[41] Work on the Norfolk dry dock at the Gosport Navy Yard started the following November 1827. Baldwin traveled between the two sites leaving these men in charge of the construction in his absence.

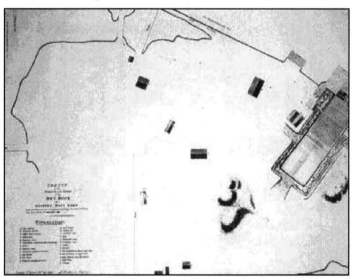

Figure 2 - "Sketch of the Position of the Works of the Dry Dock" as it was on November 1, 1829 at the Gosport Navy Yard, Portsmouth, Virginia. (National Archives)

Figure (2) is from the original drawing at the National Archives and shows the status of work of the excavation of the dry dock at the Gosposrt Navy Yard and the layout of the support buildings in the yard as of November 1, 1829. Loammi Baldwin signed this drawing on November 27, 1829.

The first step of the required excavation was the installation of a cofferdam to protect the site from the waters of the Elizabeth River.

> "Double rows of sheet piling, spaced 8 to 13 feet apart, were driven into the harbor mud, and the space between was filled with loose stone and earth in order to resist the considerable lateral thrust of tidal forces."[42]

Figure (3) is a close-up of the dry dock excavation portion of this sketch, which also shows the status of the timber piles that had been driven into the floor of the dock by November 1, 1829. These wooden piles were necessary to support the granite stone and eventual weight of the ships to be drydocked. This status sketch is very detailed and is virtually a work of art.

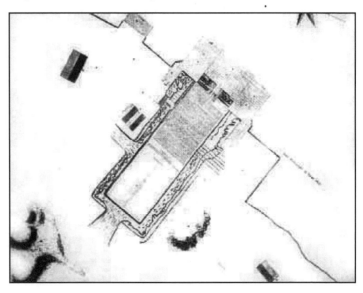

Figure 3 - Close-up of excavation status of the first dry dock constructed in United States. This drawing depicted the status of excavation as of November 1, 1829. (National Archives)

Figure (4) is a close-up of the title block for this sketch. It provides the legend for the buildings and excavation features shown on the sketch. Included is the listing of the slopes for

16

wheeling out the earth and the chute for the stones. The title block also provides a close up Loammi Baldwin's signature.

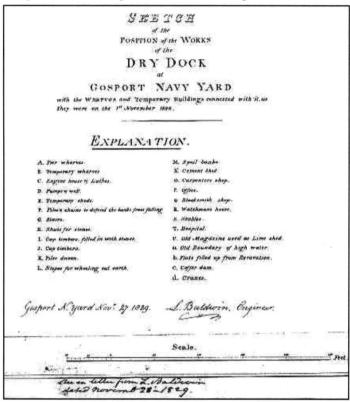

Figure 4 - Close-up of the explanation section of November 27, 1829 excavation and Gosport Navy Yard "Sketch of the Position of the Works of the Dry Dock". The engineer was Loammi Baldwin whose signature appears on this sketch. (National Archives)

Other revealing aspects of the sketch include the reference to the use of cement and the essential ingredient of lime making this design state-of-the-art for its time. A stable and a blacksmith shop were also required, as beasts of burden were used to haul the earth, stones, and piles around the yard. A pump house was also noted, as steam driven pumps to pump the water out of the dock made construction of this dry dock possible.

The tide change alone in the Elizabeth River, into which this dry dock opens, was insufficient to support the drydocking of ships-of-the-line. The invention of the steam engine and the associated pumping mechanism were the most important inventions that led to the utility of the stone (graving) docks for these larger ships. In 1797, England was the first to use steam engines to pump out a graving dock. According to the U.S. Navy's Naval History Division in regard to this first dry dock at the Gosport Navy Yard:

> "Its pumping machinery (was) operated by steam. All American Navy (Yards) were fitted with heaving down wharves but only the Norfolk Yard had a dry dock at that time."[43]

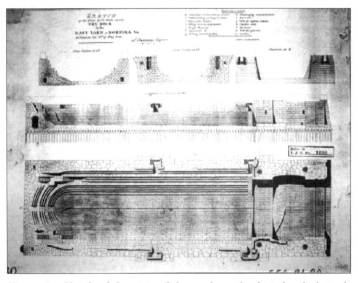

Figure 5 - Sketch of the state of the work on the first dry dock in the United States at the Gosport Navy Yard near Norfolk, Virginia as it was on May 10, 1832. (National Archives)

The drawing shown in Figure (5) shows the construction progress of this dock as of May 10, 1832. Dry dock construction at that time was still on going and had a full year of construction yet to come. The stone installation was not yet complete, which is seen in the gaps in the top of the cross section and profile views.

The dry dock gates were not yet installed. Engineer Baldwin was still in charge of construction as evidenced by his signature on this drawing.

Figure (6) Is a sketch of the status of work on the nearly completed Gosport dry dock with the gates now in place on November 2, 1832. The stone work was almost completed at this point. The dry dock opened seven months later.

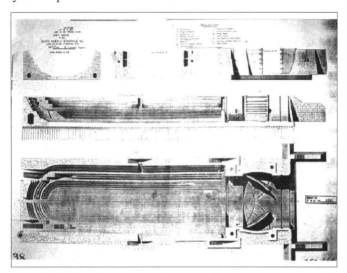

Figure 6 - Sketch of the status of work on the near completed dry dock with the gates in place at the Gosport Navy Yard near Norfolk, Virginia as it was on November 2, 1832. (National Archives)

The dry dock gate pictured in Figure (7), was designed so it could be opened after the dry dock had been flooded to the current tide level. After the ship was hauled into the dry dock, the gates were closed and the water was pumped out using a steam engine and pumps. The gate was opened and closed using a chain and capstan mechanism. This huge gate was later replaced by a caisson as the method for keeping water out of the dock.

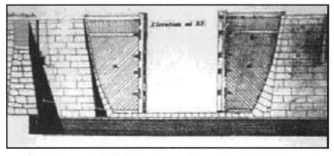

Figure 7 - Gate at the entrance to the Gosport Dry dock as it was on November 2, 1832. (National Archives).

When this stone dry dock was finally completed, it was 319' 5" long and 86' 3" wide with a mean low water level over the blocks of 17' 5 ¾".[44] The first drydocking in the United States occurred in this dock on June 17, 1833, as shown in the lithograph in Figure (8). The ship was the *USS DELAWARE*.[45] This date was chosen because it was the anniversary of the Battle of Bunker Hill in which Loammi Baldwin's father fought.

> "The gates of the Navy's first dry dock, at the Norfolk Navy Yard, swing open on June 17, 1833, to admit the *DELAWARE, 74*, to have her bottom recoppered. ... When steam driven pumps emptied the dock, the *DELAWARE* settled in perfect alignment."[46]

There is an inscription in the wall at the end of this dry dock that can still be seen today, which was inscribed in 1933 to commemorate the 100th anniversary of the opening of this first dry dock in the United States. This inscription states that the President of the United States, when this dry dock commenced construction in 1827, was John Quincy Adams and the President of the United States when the dry dock was completed in 1833 was Andrew Jackson. The dry dock was officially completed in March 1834. This dry dock is still inside the fenced Industrial Controlled Area (ICA) of the present Norfolk Naval Shipyard and still sees use today. Obviously, this dry dock should always be preserved as a monument to early American naval and industrial history and eventually be opened to the general public.

Loammi Baldwin's superbly designed dry docks stand today as a tribute to his genius and attention to detail. Loammi Baldwin II was also made a Colonel, like his father before him, a tribute to a project where the two largest civil works of the time were underway simultaneously using the same working plans.[47]

> "Baldwin designed and constructed two superb facilities whose functional success established a prototype on which many of the Navy's future dry dock installations were based."[48]

The Gosport dry dock alone cost $974,365.65 in 1827 and took six years to build. When the *USS DELAWARE* drydocked on June 17, 1833, there was great fanfare, as captured by Mr. J. G. Bruff's lithograph, shown in Figure (8). This lithograph was dedicated to the dry dock architect, Engineer Loammi Baldwin, by Mr. Bruff. It is obvious that Mr. Bruff had great admiration for Loammi Baldwin's masterpiece and the enormity of the event as evidenced by this beautifully detailed lithograph.

Figure 8 - *USS DELAWARE entering the Gosport Dry dock at Norfolk June 17, 1833.*[49] *This was the first drydocking in the United States. (Naval Historical Center)*

Mr. Bruff indeed captured a great moment for still a young nation. The successful construction of this dry dock, capable of providing essential repair service to ships-of-the-line, was quite a notable achievement for the time. This was the greatest such facility ever built to date in the Western Hemisphere. President Jackson visited the Gosport Yard and the *DELAWARE* on the July 29, 1833, prior to the ship leaving for New York after her hull repairs were completed.[50] The *USS DELAWARE* deployed to the Mediterranean after visiting New York.

Mr. Bruff's lithograph is quite enlightening as to how this docking actually occurred. First, it suggests that the U.S. Naval officers in charge of this drydocking knew something of ship stability as the yardarms of *DELAWARE* were placed in their lowest position. This action lowered the ship's center of gravity, increasing the overall stability of the ship as it landed on the dry dock blocks. The figure also shows how the ship was hauled into the dry dock. There is a head-line running from the *DELAWARE's* bow to the head capstan at the end of the dry dock. This capstan was manned by seven or eight sailors who used human power to haul the ship into the dry dock. Poles were placed into the top of the capstan, and the men walked around the capstan pushing on the poles.

Figure (9) is another lithograph by Mr. Bruff showing the *DELAWARE* fully positioned in the dry dock after the water in the dock was pumped out. Several additional observations can be made from this most complete depiction of what happened that fateful day in 1833.

From an engineering viewpoint, the artist has actually answered many questions. The second of two lithographs made of this event, Figure (9) shows that "wale shores" were used to support the ship while in dry dock. Wale shores are poles placed horizontally between the dry dock stone wall and the sides of the ship. These shores were most likely arranged to correspond to the frames of the ship's hull. It also shows steam powered ships in the background that probably were the port tugs that brought the *DELAWARE* up the Elizabeth River to the Yard, and assisted in the docking of the ship. The lithograph also shows a closer view of the lowered yards (yardarms) which increased the ship's stability.

Having the masts still in place and the yards lowered but not removed, was a major advantage of this type of dry dock. Up to this point, ships had to be hauled up marine railways to remove them from the water. The capacity of the marine railways were such that required weight to be removed and stability increased. This necessitated the removal of topside weights such as the masts and yards.

Marines were used to keep the crowd back from the dry dock. It was a grand occasion including the attendance by dignitaries and ladies in grand apparel with umbrellas to keep off the hot June sun.

> "The ceremonies, in keeping with the importance of the occasion, were attended by many national and local dignitaries as well as attracted widespread attention."[51]

This dry dock, now called Dry Dock Nr. 1 at Norfolk Naval Shipyard, is still being used in 2003, over 170 years after it was built. The Commander of Norfolk Naval Shipyard, Captain Tim

Scheib, USN, stated in January 1998 that Dry Dock Nr. 1 is the tightest (leaks the least) of all his eight dry docks. This is a tremendous tribute to the design genius of Loammi Baldwin and the craftsmanship of his workforce.

Figure 9 – "USS DELAWARE in the Gosport Dry dock at Norfolk 17 June 1833".[52] (Naval Historical Center)

Baldwin's other stone dry dock, at the old Charlestown Navy Yard near Boston, was completed one week after the Stone Dry dock at Gosport in 1833. The first ship dry docked in the Boston dry dock was the *USS CONSTITUTION*. This dry dock, too, is still being used in 2003 for the occasional drydocking of the *USS CONSTITUTION* and other historical vessels and is part of the Department of Interior's National Historic Park. David Stevenson, a Scottish engineer, visited the United States in 1837 and made this comment about the graving docks at Norfolk and Boston ...

> "the finest specimens of masonry which I met with in America".[53]

Chapter 5

A New Dry Dock at the New York Navy Yard — Largest in the World

The need for more graving docks persisted. The Scottish engineer, David Stevenson, made this observation in 1837 about ship repair facilities in the U.S. ...

> "There was a want of proper accommodations for vessels requiring repair."[54]

In 1835, Loammi Baldwin II left his recently completed dry dock projects in Norfolk and Boston and commenced the surveys for yet a third graving dock at New York. This study was at the direction of the Honorable Mahlon Dickerson, Secretary of the Navy. Figure (10) is the legend from this survey drawing, completed in 1835.

Baldwin's survey ended up being very close to the site selected for what was later to be the largest dry dock in the world – the Granite Dry Dock at the New York Navy Yard. The site chosen was at the northeast corner of the Navy Yard. One of the interesting aspects of this survey, considering it was 1835, is that borings were conducted up to eighty feet in depth. The borings brought up sand and clay plus fresh water. No rock was found. It was determined however, that "a dry dock may be safely founded".[55]

In July 1837, the world's largest and most heavily armed man-of-war was launched at the Philadelphia Navy Yard. The *USS PENNSYLVANIA* shown in Figure (11) was a 120-gun ship-of-the-line, designed by Joshua Humphreys' son, Samuel. A crowd, estimated at 100,000 witnessed the launching.[56] This ship was the impetus that led to the construction of the dry dock at New York Navy Yard that began construction in 1841. The increased site of ship construction led to the construction of larger graving docks.

PLAN
of the
Soundings & Examinations
of
WALLABOUT BAY
for a
Dry Dock
in the
Navy Yard at Brooklyn,
New York.
Made in May 1835 by direction of the
Hon. Mahlon Dickerson, Secretary of the Navy.

By
L. Baldwin, Engineer

Figure 10 - Title of the first Plan for a Dry Dock at New York. (National Archives)

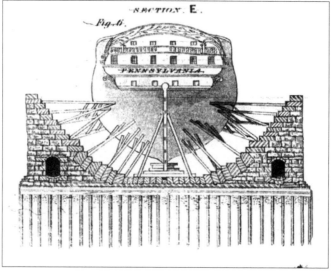

Figure 11 - USS PENNSYLVANIA depicted in new dry dock at New York Navy Yard. (Naval Historical Center)

Charles B. Stuart, Engineer-in-Chief of the United States Navy, wrote a book in 1852 entitled *The Naval Dry Docks from the United States*. That volume was primarily his personal testimonial of the details of the design and construction of the New York dry dock. Stuart had overall responsibility for the New York dry dock effort. The book, however, did describe all the U.S. Naval dry docks at the time.[57]

He dedicated this book to his "sincere friend" Millard Fillmore, President of the United States.[58] Figure (12) is the dedication page from the book.

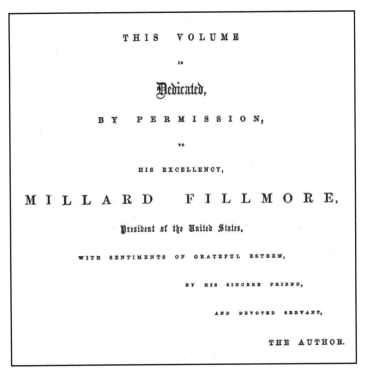

Figure 12 - Dedication page of Charles B. Stuart's 1852 book to President Fillmore. (Naval Historical Center)

Preliminary work did not begin on the drydock at the New York Navy Yard until 1841, and it was not completed until ten years later. Not only was this a major engineering project. It soon became one of extraordinary difficulty, when it was discovered that the foundations had to be laid on a deep layer of quicksand 37 feet below mean tide.

William J. McAlpine, who was appointed chief engineer of the project in February 1846, remained in charge of the dry dock construction until October 1849. It was under his leadership that the cofferdam, excavation of the bottom pit, pile driving, timber and concrete installation, drydock super structure, pump well and engine house were completed. This established McAlpine as one of the leading engineers of the time.[59] According to Charles Stuart, the credit for completing this massive civil work should go to Engineer McAlpine.

This dry dock, which ended up costing two million dollars in 1850, required eighty thousand tons of stone. It was 350 feet long and could accommodate the largest war steamers afloat at the time.[60]

Figure (13) is a close-up of a sketch from the National Archives showing the progress of construction of the this dry dock as it was on October 1, 1848. The sketch also shows cross-sectional views of the dry dock.

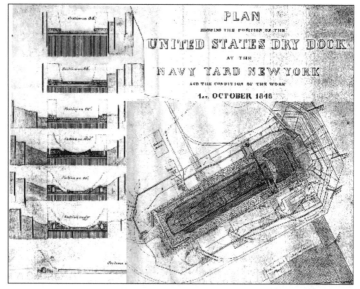

Figure 13 - Drawing of the status of work of the United States Dry dock in New York as of October 1, 1848. (National Archives).

The cross sectional views of the dry dock [left side of Figure (13)] show that at this point in October 1848, all the pilings for the dock floor had been driven. Notice the piles extend all the way under the dock walls. Wall construction was less than 50 percent completed at this point.

In Figure (14) a Cement House and the Engineer's Office for dry dock construction is shown. Directly next to the dry dock, Engine House No. 3 and a Tool House are shown. The Engine House was one of the pumping stations for the drainage tunnel of the dry dock.

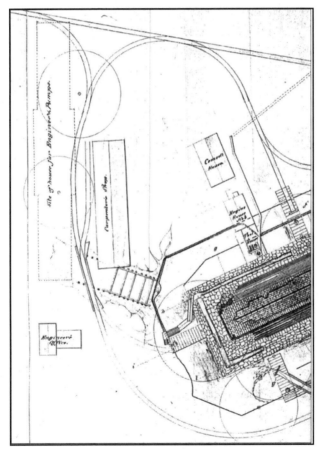

Figure 14 - This is a close-up view of the New York Dry dock and surrounding area on October 1, 1848 showing the site of the building for the engines and pumps. (National Archives)

Figure (14) is a close-up view of the same sketch shown in Figure (13). This view shows the associated buildings to be constructed around the dry dock, including a house for Engines & Pumps [upper left side of Figure (14)]. Figure (15) is a sketch of the engine house.[61] This engine house was 300 feet long with an iron and copper roof over the entire building.

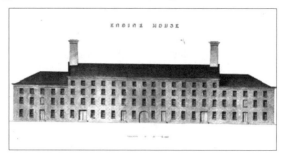

F*igure 15 - Drawing of the engine house adjacent to the New York dry dock. (Naval Historical Center)*

Figure (16) shows a plan view of the dry dock, along with part of the engine house foundation and the associated pump-well, receiving and discharge culverts.[62] Figure (17) is an inside view of the engine house showing:

> "a side elevation of the engine, the engine frame, and the interior side of the engine room: also, the reservoir chamber, with air-pump, condenser, and air-chamber; the pumps, suction pipes, and valves; connecting air-pipe, and columns to support the reservoir and engine bed-plates, the pump covers and connections, the balance-wheel and working-beam and a longitudinal section of the pump-well, with iron flooring over the masonry."[63] This pumping mechanism was designed to dewater the dry dock as rapidly as possible. No pumping facility of this magnitude had previously been built anywhere in the United States. Engineer McAlpine presented to a Naval Board a design that consisted of an engine with two lifting pumps, each fifty inches in diameter.

This design was approved with some modifications, on March 21, 1849, by this Board which included Charles W. Copeland, a steam engineer in the naval service; William M. Ellis, engineer and machinist from the Washington Navy Yard; and Engineer McAlpine. Construction of the pumping machinery was contracted out to Gouveneur Kemble of Cold Spring, New York.

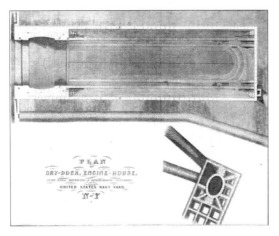

Figure 16 - Graving dock at New York Navy Yard plan view and the pump well, receiving, and discharge culverts. (Naval Historical Center)

Figure 17 - Side elevation of Engine and Pumps and Longitudinal Section of Well. (Naval Historical Center).

Another interesting aspect of the construction of this dry dock was the design and construction of both a caisson and a gate system. Figure (18) is a drawing showing the design of the culvert gate mechanism. This valve was hand operated using a hallow shaft, right angle drive, and lifting chain to open the culverts to flooding.

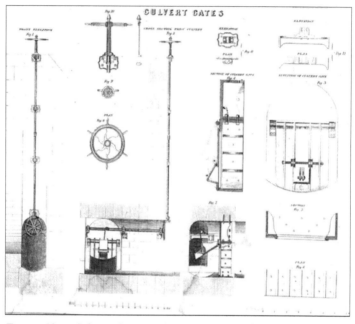

Figure 18 - Culvert Gate mechanism for the New York Dry Dock. (Naval Historical Center)

Figure (19) is an 1849 isometric drawing of this stone graving dock that was to become Dry Dock Nr. 1 at New York Navy Yard. This isometric view shows the enormous number of piles required to support this dry dock. The construction and installation was completed to support the drydocking of the frigate *USS ST. LAWRENCE,* on January 16, 1851. The water from the dry dock was successfully removed in two hours and ten minutes. The dry dock was 349 feet long, almost 30 feet longer than the Charlestown Gosport graving docks. [64]

Figure (20) is the final completed side view of the New York graving dock, along with various sectional views. The figure also shows the *USS PENNSYLVANIA* in the graving dock, the largest ship in the Navy at the time. Charles Stuart describes this figure:

> "showing the outline of the ship of the line *"Pennsylvania,"* the largest man-of-war in the navy, if not the world; the stern of the same vessel is [also seen]. At the end of this section, is seen the culvert, in the masonry of the Dock, through which water passes from the chamber of the Dock to the pump-well. The steps and slides for timber are also exhibited ... at the head of the Dock. At the lower end is the groove in the masonry to receive the stem and keel of the floating gate. Near the stern of the *"Pennsylvania,"* are steps leading from the coping of the Dock to the broad altar of the chamber, also, the opening or entrance to the draining culvert. The foundation timbers, piling, and concrete, are seen in this and other figures in sections."[65]

Figure 19 - This is an 1849 isometric drawing of the graving dock that was to become Dry Dock Nr. 1 at what became the Brooklyn Navy Yard, New York. (National Archives)

Charles Stuart made the following tribute to the engineers that summarized the tremendous achievement in the completion of this dry dock at New York Navy Yard:

"Its successful completion is as much to be attributed to the untiring industry, skill, and watchfulness of the superintending engineers, and their able assistants, as to the admirable plans and principles upon which it is built, and will remain for the ages, one of the proudest monuments of the engineering, and mechanical skill of the nineteenth century."[66]

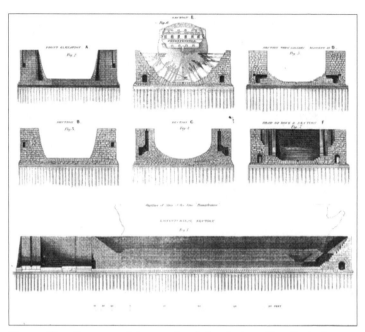

Figure 20 - Drawing of the completed dry dock at New York showing cross sections (one with USS PENNSYLVANIA in dock) and side view. (Naval Historical Center)

In parallel with this expansion of Navy Yard dry docks, Secretary Dickerson also pushed for and succeeded in advancing steam propulsion aboard naval vessels. Steam power soon after became the center point of naval engineering.

On July 12, 1836, Charles H. Haswell, the designer of the first steam engines for use by the Navy on *FULTON II*, became the first engineer commissioned in the U.S. Navy. He later became engineer-in-chief. In 1837 steam powered *FULTON II* was launched. This was the beginning of the steam Navy of the United States.[67] This change to steam later lead to much larger ships and the need for even larger dry docks.

With ever expanding navy yards and the growing requirement for these yards to be able to accommodate more sophisticated repairs, on August 31, 1842, the Bureau of Yards and Docks was established.[68] Steam powered engines and pumps became the backbone of the navy yards.

Chapter 6

More Dry Docks Emerge and Dry Docks on the West Coast Emerge

At the Portsmouth Navy Yard, in New Hampshire, the requirement to have a ship repair capacity became increasingly apparent. This need first arose in 1826; however, Congress did not approve a dry dock to be located in Portsmouth until many years later.[69]

> "Years of agitation and lobbying were to follow before authorization could be obtained by Congress. In 1848, a survey team recommended a floating dry dock and basin would be more suitable for the Portsmouth Yard than one blasted out of rock. . In 1851, a contract was entered into to construct, with all the necessary machinery and appendages, a Floating Balance dry dock and Marine Railway. It was tested and accepted in June, 1852."[70]

This wooden floating dry dock was to first see service in a Navy Yard and was put into service in 1852.[71] In fact, this was the earliest known true floating dry dock. It had hollow sidewalls and a hollow pontoon that lifted the ship entirely above the water.[72] This was the beginning of the U.S. Navy's extensive use of floating dry docks, which still continues today. Two years later, in 1854, another floating dry dock was put into service at the Mare Island Yard in California. This will be discussed in detail later.

> "[The Portsmouth floating dry dock] was constructed on Pierce's Island, opposite the Navy Yard, and then floated across the river. It was 350 feet long and 105 feet 4 inches wide outside, with walls 38 feet high."[73]

As with all the floating dry docks of the time, it had a boiler on each wing wall geared to pumps. In this case, the boilers produced 50 horsepower and drove twelve pumps.

> "These pumps raised 17,418 tons of water per hour and were capable of raising a ship of 5000 tons."[74]

Like the first dry dock at the Norfolk (Gosport) Navy Yard, the first ship drydocked in the floating dry dock at the Portsmouth Navy Yard was a 74-gun ship-of-the-line. The ship was the *USS FRANKLIN,* which had been constructed in Philadelphia 40 years earlier. She displaced 2257 tons. The smaller *USS CONSTITUTION* was also hauled out of the water at Portsmouth Navy Yard in 1854. However, in this case, the marine railway was used.

According to a photograph of the *CONSTITUTION* on the Portsmouth Navy Yard marine railway in 1854, her masts and yards were removed prior to the ship being hauled out of the water. This is an indication that the marine railway was at or near capacity with *CONSTITUTION*. Most likely, ships-of-the-line exceeded the capacity of the marine railway and could not be hauled out of the water in this fashion. This gave credence to the need for a floating dry dock with a larger capacity.

This floating dry dock at Portsmouth saw active service until she was sold on May 18, 1907. The basin for the floating dry dock later became the site of the first graving dock at the Portsmouth Navy Yard.

With the end of the Mexican War and the occupation of California in 1847-1848, the discovery of gold in 1849, and the resulting rush of travelers to California, Western expansion of United States naval repair facilities was urgently required. The response by Congress was almost immediate. On September 28, 1850, Congress authorized the Secretary of the Navy to contract for the construction of a floating dry dock in California.

In 1852, the Navy authorized the construction of this floating dry dock which would be built on Mare Island. The dry dock would also require a shore facility. Thus the birth of the Mare Island Navy Yard, the first Navy Yard on the West Coast located near what is now Vallejo, California at the Northernmost part of San Francisco Bay. The plans for the floating drydock were completed by Charles B. Stuart, Engineer-in-Chief of the Navy, and sent to the Secretary of the Navy in April, 1851.

This floating dry dock for Mare Island was built in New York, then broken down into components which were loaded on four ships that sailed around Cape Horn to San Francisco Bay and Mare

Island. The following is an account of the construction and shipment of this floating dry dock to California:

> "On May 19th, 1852, the Navy contracted with Samuel D. Dakin, Rutherford Moody, John S. Gilbert, and Zeno Secor, all of New York, to build the dock within two years from the date, at a cost of $610,000. The design called for eleven individual sections, each 100 feet long and 32 feet wide, with two end floats to each section. Six pumps were installed on each section, with a total capacity of 1800 gallons per minute. Power for the pumps was supplied by four steam engines, which, with their boilers ... situated on small houses perched atop each end of the floats. The dock was built at the foot of Fifteenth Street, on the North River, where work commenced in June, 1851, and was finished ... spring ... [1852]. .... After having been assembled in New York, the dock was knocked down, all the pieces properly numbered, and the long voyage around Cape Horn to California began. First shipment was made on the ship *EMPIRE*, which reached San Francisco on August 13, 1852.... The rest of the material made the trip on three ...ships: ... *DEFIANCE*, *QUEEN OF THE EAST*, and *CALIFORNIA PACKET*."[75]

Figure (21) is photo of the original construction drawing of this floating dry dock. In this figure, the deck house containing the mechanical drives can be seen. This is an end view and top view of one of the eleven sections of this sectional floating dry dock. The wing walls are the structures on either side of the dry dock deck. The walls contain a float (airbox) and pumping mechanisms. On the deck are the side blocks that could be hauled into place once the ship landed on the centerline keel blocks.

Figure (22) is a close-up of the top of one section of the floating dry dock wing wall. It shows the mechanism for raising and lowering the float located in each wing wall. The figure also illustrates a shaft running longitudinally across the top of the wing wall. This shaft is powered by a steam engine located on top of another section near the boiler. The shaft was coupled together at each section of the dry dock, and powered a right angle drive via a reduction gear that in turn powered a vertical shaft. This same shaft also powered two reciprocating pump mechanisms on each section of the dry dock via a belt drive.

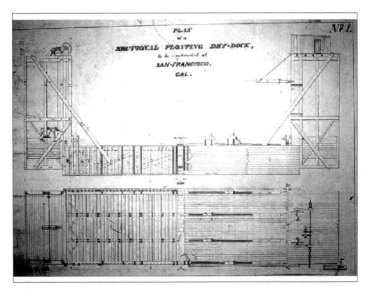

Figure 21 - Construction drawing of the first dry dock on the West Coast of the United States. Drawing dated May 19, 1851. (National Archives)

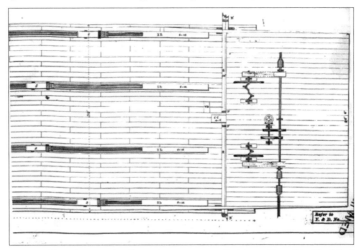

Figure 22 - Top view looking down on top of wing wall and half of dock floor on one section of the first sectional floating dry dock at Mare Island Navy Yard. (National Archives)

Figure (23) is another close-up of the cross sectional view of the dry dock wingwall. The vertical shaft, powered from the top of the dock section via a right angle drive, drove another right angle drive and a pinion gear which in turn drove a much larger gear which was located directly over the top of the float. This large gear drove a shaft with a ratcheting mechanism on either end of the shaft. The float could be pushed down by this mechanism. These floats were used to keep the dock level during a docking or undocking evolution.

This mechanism was on each wingwall of the dry dock. They were operated at exactly the same time by the shaft coupling in order to keep the dry dock level. Employing this clever method — but crude by today's standards — this must have been an interesting sight to watch. The slightest hang up of any of the shaft and gear alignments would have immediately put a list on the dry dock.

All section floats were pushed down simultaneously. The sections were linked by topside shafts that were coupled together. The floats were really empty tanks, and had to stay dry to work. A power take-off belt was used to drive a lever system that drove a vertical shaft up and down that was connected to pumps in each pontoon section. The dry dock was lowered by flooding the pontoon deck main tank, and was raised by pumping water out of these tanks.

Theodore D. Wilson, Assistant Naval Constructor, U.S. Navy, wrote the following description of the how this floating dry dock worked in 1873. At that time he was an instructor of naval construction at the U.S. Naval Academy in Annapolis, Maryland:

> "There is placed in each end-frame, at either side of a section, a float connected with four posts of the framework, by two shafts with small cog-wheels on each end, which work into pinions properly fastened upon one side of each of these posts, by which machinery raises the end-floats when lowering the sections, and forces them down when raising a vessel; they serve as an equilibrium power, to keep the ends of the main tanks on a level. ... At the end of each main tank are one single and one double pump, which, together with the floats, are operated by an engine situated each side and on top of the sections. The shafting which conveys the power of the engines from one section to another, runs into a hollow sliding-shaft ... Between the sections there is a universal joint in the shaft, to provide for any deflection there may be in the line of shafting extending along and over the platform."[76]

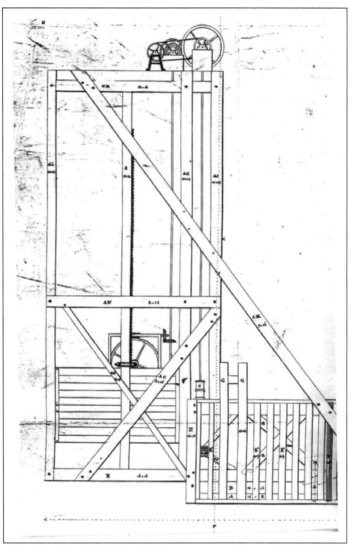

Figure 23 - Close-up of the end view looking longitudinally at one of the Mare Island floating dry dock wingwall and ballast tank sections. (National Archives)

Figure (24) is a cross sectional view of the dry dock floor. It shows the side blocks and keel blocks profile. This dry dock used hauled side blocks almost exactly as they are used today. The side block caps had a "universal" shape so they could be used for different ships with varying hull dimensions.

The side blocks sat on a track. Not shown in the drawing is the method by which the side blocks were hauled. This was probably a chain mechanism fair lead to the top of the wing walls via sheaves, a method still in use today. The chain would be pulled and all side blocks would be hauled in on either side of the ship.

When the dock was submerged, the ship was hauled in the dry dock. The "graduated" wale shores were then swung out to center the ship in the dock over the keel blocks. The wooden side block assemblies became buoyant and the assembly would be relatively easy to pull inward toward the ship's hull. When the ship landed on the keel blocks, the side blocks were inhauled to the hull. As the side block assemblies were hauled in, a steel plate or "paul" followed, falling into the rack track, over which the side blocks were floating. This prevented the side blocks from slipping back out once contact was made with the hull. The side block assembly was prevented from floating more than an inch or two over this track by "L" shaped brackets. This track or "weir" with the rack on top of it was "I" shaped so the "L" braces could slip beneath it holding the side block assembly, thus preventing complete float off. The "L" brackets were nailed or lag screwed into the sides of the wooden side block assembly structure.

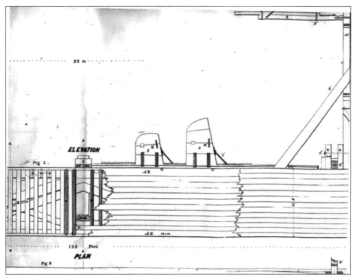

Figure 24 - Close-up of the end view looking longitudinally at one of the Mare Island floating dry dock floor sections. (National Archives)

Theodore Wilson describes the docking evolution, including how the floats and main tank in pontoon are operated:

> "When a vessel is to be docked, the main tank is filled with enough water to admit of sinking it, the end-floats are run up as the dock sinks down, and their speed regulated so as to keep it level at all times. When the keel-blocks have been submerged a foot or two more than the draft of the vessel to be docked, the ship is hauled in and placed by the graduated wale-shores in the center of the dock. The pumps are started and the floats worked down until the keel-blocks have a bearing on the keel of the ship. The engine is now stopped, and the workmen pass rapidly from one section to another on the platforms, and by means of ropes reaching each platform, haul the bilge-blocks now under water, with great facility, against the bilge of the ship. The pumps and floats are now set to work until the deck of the dock is raised above the water."[77]

Also seen in Figure (24) at the top is the graduated wale shore. This shore was designed to swing out from the side of the wing wall once the ship was in position in the dock and landed on the blocks. It was projected out until it came into contact with the side of the ship. This shore also had a ratcheting mechanism to prevent the shore from backing out, thus maintaining solid contact with the ship. This shore was a method to align the ship and keep the ship from overturning in the dry dock once landed.

Once the floating dry dock at Mare Island neared completion, the Navy Yard itself opened in 1854. David Farragut, who later became the Navy's first admiral, commanded the Yard. As a preliminary test of several sections of the dry dock, the steamer *PACIFIC* was raised. However, the first official drydocking was on September 21, 1854 and the ship was the *USS WARREN*. Mare Island Navy Yard had opened one week earlier.

> "Farragut was anxious to witness the operations of the sectional dock which had been brought out from New York in 1852, so preparations were made for docking the *WARREN* on September 20, 1854. Due to lack of sufficient water over the dock floor, the docking was postponed until the following day [September 21, 1854],

when the *WARREN* was taken upon the dock in seventy minutes flat."[78]

The first drydocking on the West Coast had been accomplished. The United States had thus taken the dramatic step of significantly extending its ship repair facilities across the continent. This symbolized the growth in United States' maritime power and quickly played a key role in the maintenance of the Pacific Squadron.

"In a report dated November 1, 1854, the Chief of the Bureau of Yards and Docks stated that by April 20 of that year [1854], the dock had taken up seventeen ships, including the *USS PORTSMOUTH*, and *USS WARREN*."[79]

The first repair job that required drydocking was the *USS ST MARY'S*, a 22-gun sloop of the Pacific Squadron. The ship arrived at Mare Island February 13, 1855.[80] She was one of the first ships the United States Navy stationed on the West Coast. She was 149 feet long and displaced 950 long tons.

The *USS PORTSMOUTH,* a 20-gun sloop-of-war, also of the Pacific Squadron pictured in Figure (25), was one of Mare Island's first floating dry dock customers. This ship had made history eight years earlier on the July 9, 1846 when she captured San Francisco from Mexico using a seventy man landing party. This ship was also the first ship my grandfather, Commander Joseph F. Daniels, USN, served on in 1891, which shows how long these sailing warships stayed in service.

The floating dry dock was not only critical to maintaining the eight United States Naval vessels in the Pacific in 1854. It also serviced the vastly larger number of merchant and foreign vessels that frequented California. In fact, the dry dock itself was a significant draw for ships to frequent San Francisco Bay, thus bringing trade to the area.

At the time, trade and communication between the East and West coasts of the United States depended primarily on merchant vessels. These ships dominated the docking list of the dry dock at Mare Island. Thus, this floating dry dock played a key role in the development of the West.

Figure 25 - USS PORTSMOUTH. One of the first ships drydocked in the floating dry dock at the Mare Island Navy Yard. (National Archives)

After the floating dry dock was operational at Mare Island in 1854, the Navy wanted expanded facilities at Mare Island. The Navy contracted the California Dry Dock Company to construct a basin and a marine railway.[81]

Chapter 7

Naval Repair Facility Expansion Plans Continued on the East Coast

As well as the Navy, Congress had interest in expanding the East Coast drydocking capabilities in 1847. On March 3, 1847, Congress authorized the Secretary of the Navy to pursue construction of floating dry docks at the Navy Yards at Portsmouth, Philadelphia, and Pensacola. Fifty thousand dollars was approved for the dock at Philadelphia. On August 3, 1848, Congress further enacted appropriations for the floating dry docks at these three yards, and directed the Secretary of the Navy:

> "... forthwith, to enter into a contract with Samuel D. Dakin and Rutherford Moody, for complete construction, within a reasonable time from the date of the contract, of a Sectional floating Dry Dock, basin, and railways at the Navy Yard at Philadelphia, according to the plan and specifications submitted by them to the Navy Department."[82]

Samuel D. Dakin and Rutherford Moody were the same gentlemen who were contracted to build the sectional dry dock for Mare Island discussed in the previous chapter. Congress had an interest in making sure these new floating dry docks could accommodate war steamers of the largest class. Congress, in the Act approved on August 3, 1848, specified that the docks accommodate steamers 350 feet in length. $400,000 was appropriated in this act for these works. Congress appropriated an additional $351,240 on September 28, 1850.

The reason for this Congressional interest was to the introduction of the steamship into the fleet. Steamship construction kicked into high gear in the 1840s. These ships of higher displacement and increased length and beam dimensions required even larger dry docks to accomplish repairs.

> "Steamships gained popularity in the 1840s. One private yard, Theodore Birely & Son, in Kensington, Pennsylvania, built 107 steamers in 10 years."[83]

"A Wilmington [Delaware] firm, Betts, Harlan & Hollingsworth, built the first twin-screw, oceangoing iron steamer in 1845. For a dozen years after that, Wilmington produced more iron tonnage in shipbuilding than any other city in the United States. Philadelphia was second."[84]

The construction of a sectional floating dry dock for Philadelphia commenced in December 1849 and was completed June 5, 1851. This dry dock shown in Figure (26) consisted of nine sections, three being thirty feet wide and six being thirty-two feet wide.

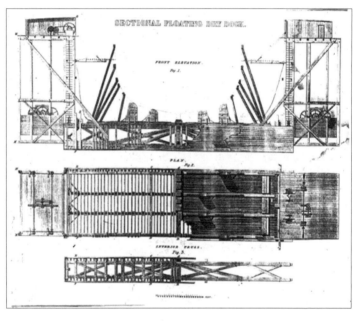

Figure 26 - Drawing of Philadelphia Sectional Dry Dock completed June 5th 1851. (Naval Historical Center)

Each section had a main tank, two end frames, and two end floats. Longitudinal and transverse truss frames were placed in each main tank. Timbers in the trusses were bound together by large iron bands. A primary consideration of the design was to give the transverse center of the main tank enough support where the keel of the vessel was to rest. Two timbers were placed under this point as well as additional timbers on the deck six inches thick. This gave a total of three feet of timber support under the keel-blocks.

Bilge blocks were also placed on the dry dock floor. They were centered over trusses over which the side blocks slid.[85] The side blocks were hauled in until they touched the hull of the vessel being drydocked.

This dry dock was the same design as that used for the Mare Island dry dock. Again, the purpose of the float or tanks in each side of the dry dock's sections was to provide additional buoyancy to the sections and serve as equilibrium power to keep either side of each section in a level position.

When this dry dock was used, only the sections of the dry dock necessary to lift the vessel were actually employed. They were joined together by connecting beams, keyed so as to make the several sections equivalent to one structure.

The assembled dimensions of the dry dock produced a floor that was more than three hundred feet long and one hundred five feet wide. This sectional dry dock also had the capacity to dock one of its own sections for repair (self-docking).

The final cost of the sectional dock in 1851 was as follows: for the woodwork and machinery of six sections, 32 feet wide, at $41,206.96 each the total came to $247,241.76; for the wood-work and machinery of three sections, 30 feet wide, at $38,860.31 each the total came to $116,580.93. The grand total was $363,822.69.[86]

In each side of the dry dock were located four steam engines. Two engines were twenty-horsepower and two were twelve horsepower. Each had an associated locomotive boiler. These engines provided power to three pumps at each end of the section and the end float mechanism. Shafting conveyed the power from one section to another. Universal joints were used in the shafting between the dry dock sections to allow for any deflections in the line of the shafting.

Theodore White made a very prophetic statement in describing the utility of the floating sectional dry dock. His idea is exactly how the new floating dry dock at Bath Iron Works is designed to operate with the land level transfer facility in 2001, 128 years later:

> "If desired, the vessel can now be taken in the basin [floating dry dock] opposite a marine railway, and the vessel hauled ashore, leaving the dock clear for another vessel."[87]

Charles Stuart also made reference to this method of connecting a floating dry dock to a railway system to increase the capacity of the docking system. There was a floating sectional dry dock at Philadelphia, and his idea referred to the use of this floating dry dock with a railway system.

> "At Philadelphia, three more marine railways may be constructed on the north side of the Basin, while only two could be used on the south side, in consequence of the direction of the Port Warden's line. These railways may be built at small expense, and when completed, the same Floating Dock and Hydraulic-Cylinder now used, could be used in connection with them. Thus, at but little cost, the four capacities of the Philadelphia Dock would be increased to nine..."[88]

Figure (27) depicts the concept of using a floating dry dock in conjunction with a railway system.[89] This illustration shows a steamer on the floating dry dock and a ship on the railway system, plus another under construction.

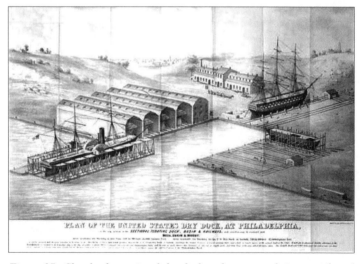

Figure 27 - Sketch of a sectional dry dock and a steamer being transferred to a land level facility. (Naval Historical Center)

As ship sizes and numbers grew, so did the need for larger graving docks. To keep up with the demand, just a few years prior to the devastating Civil War, plans for modernizing and expanding Navy Yard capabilities materialized. Figure (28), is a sketch of the proposed arrangement of pumping engines for the Gosport (Norfolk) Navy Yard that was drawn in New York on April 24, 1855. The Navy desired at this time to upgrade the early pumps installed in the first Stone Dry dock at Gosport.

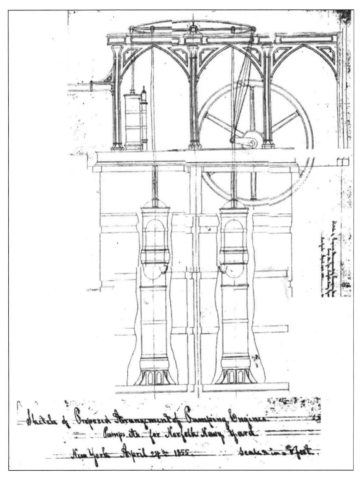

Figure 28 - Sketch of proposed arrangement of pumping engines for the Norfolk Navy Yard. Drawn in New York on April 24, 1855. (National Archives)

The pump sketch was originally to a scale of 1-inch to 1-foot that would make the circular gear shown about twelve feet in diameter. It was similar in design to that used in the graving dock at the New York Navy Yard.

A steam engine provided power to the large gear via a turning shaft. The gear provided the mechanical advantage via a rocking arm and a connecting rod to power one end of a lever. This provided the lever to its reciprocating motion. A pressure vessel with a relief valve was connected via a connection rod and piston to the other end of this lever to provide the feedback pressure to help the lever return to its original position each cycle. This up and down motion moved the pistons in the pumps via connecting rods to either side of the lever. This caused one piston to go down and one piston to go up. The piston being pulled up would draw suction from a drainage tunnel in the bottom of the dry dock. This drew water up into a crossover pipe between the two pump cylinders and into the other cylinder. At the same time, the other piston would push water into the discharge tunnel and out of the dry dock.

In 1857, plans were drawn for a proposed second dry dock at the Norfolk (Gosport) Navy Yard. These plans included estimates for replacement of the original dry docks pumping engines as well. The portion of these plans that included this estimate is shown in Figure (29). The estimate includes $60,000 for the new pumping engines and $3,000 for the removal of the pumping engines from the first dry dock.

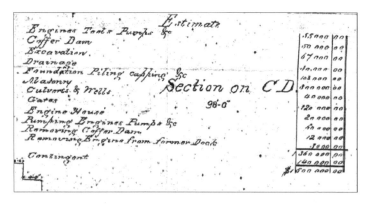

Figure 29 - Estimate of the cost of construction of a second dry dock at the Gosport Yard in 1857. (National Archives)

Table (1) is a clarification of the estimate shown in Figure (29). Interestingly enough, probably due to not having automated spreadsheets and computers that we have today let alone adding machines, there was a $10,000 error in their math for this estimate. At any rate, the estimated cost to build a second graving dock in 1857 at Norfolk was 1.5 million dollars. In today's dollars, this would be on the order of a billion dollars — a huge amount of money for a relatively poor country in 1857. This is probably why it wasn't approved until 1887. It was eventually completed in 1889.

Table 1 - 1857 estimated cost to build a second graving dock at Norfolk Navy Yard.

EQUIPMENT & LABOR ITEMS	COST ($) ESTIMATE IN 1857
Engine Tools Pumps Etc.	$55000.00
Coffer Dam	$50000.00
Excavation	$67000.00
Drainage	$40000.00
Foundation Piling capping etc.	$103000.00
Masonry	$800000.00
Culverts & Wells	$40000.00
Gates	$120000.00
Engine House	$20000.00
Pumping Engines Pumps Etc.	$60000.00
Removing Coffer Dam	$12000.00
Removing Engines from former Dock	$3000.00
Subtotal	$1,370,000.00
Contingent	$140,000.00
Total	$1,510,000.00

In Figure (30), the highest cost item (58%) was the masonry. This would include the procurement of the granite stones, transportation of these stones to Norfolk, Virginia from the Northeast, procurement of cement, and installation. Intuitively, one might think just the excavation of the graving dock would be the most labor intensive and costliest portion, as might be the case today. Excavation was only estimated at being 5% of the cost of the dry dock. Today, the environmental costs of removing and disposing of the spoilage would be tremendous.

The other two relatively high cost items were the pilings and gates. The process of driving piles in 1857 was a difficult proposition as still relatively crude steam powered pile drivers would have to be used. In addition, the dry dock gates were enormous structures requiring an extensive and costly metal fabrication process.

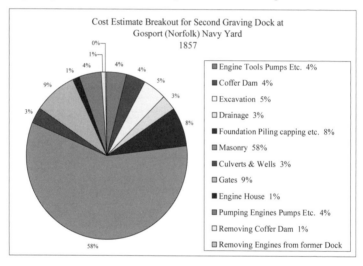

Figure 30 - Proposed 2nd dry dock at Norfolk cost estimate percentages in 1857.

However, the construction of this new graving dock at Norfolk was delayed by the Civil War. This was perhaps a blessing for the Union as the Confederates found the one dry dock at Norfolk enormously useful and eventually deadly to Union forces.

Chapter 8

The Salvaging of the *MERRIMACK* in the Norfolk (Gosport) Navy Yard Dry Dock

The stone dry dock at the Norfolk Navy Yard would again play a major — but this time deadly — role in U.S. Navy History, 28 years after this graving dock was put into service. This event changed the U.S. Navy forever and led to the ironclad ships and the end of the era of tall frigates.[90] By April 1861, this graving dock was still one of only three granite masonry dry docks in the country. The other graving docks being at Boston and New York. In addition, the Norfolk Navy Yard had the largest crane for naval work and was an important arsenal for cannons.

The Norfollk Navy Yard was largest in the United States at the time. It stretched for three-quarters of a mile along the banks of the Elizabeth River. It housed machine shops, ropewalks, ship houses, launching ways and of course the granite dry dock. In April 1861, there was a ship-of-the-line under construction in a ship-house, 3,000 cannons in the arsenal, and thousands of shells and tons of gunpowder in the magazines.[91] The 74-gun ship-of-the line *USS DELAWARE,* the same ship that was the first to be dry docked in the Stone Dry dock in 1833, was in the yard, as well as eight other ships, which included the 120-gun ship-of-the-line *USS PENNSYLVANIA* and the *USS MERRIMACK.*

The *MERRIMACK* was a steam-powered frigate that was commissioned in Annapolis, Maryland in 1856. President Franklin Pierce had attended this commissioning ceremony.[92] However, in 1861, *MERRIMACK* was laying in a state of disrepair (in ordinary) at the Norfolk Navy Yard.[93]

Captain Charles S. McCauley, an elderly Naval Officer, was the unfortunate shipyard commander in April 1861. Even though his vital and militarily lucrative shipyard was sitting only 90 miles from Richmond, Virginia; he had taken no extra precautions to guard or evacuate the facility in the event of hostilities with forces from States seceding from the Union. In April 1861,

Secretary of the Navy, Gideon Welles, wrote a letter to Captain McCauley stating:

> "It is deemed important that the steamer *MERRIMACK* should be in condition to proceed to Philadelphia or to any other yard, should it be deemed necessary."[94]

Obviously, Secretary Welles saw Philadelphia as the safer Navy Yard location for this valuable ship, which probably led him to push for a larger Navy Yard at Philadelphia immediately after the War. On April 12, 1861, Secretary Welles ordered the Chief Engineer of the Navy, Benjamin Franklin Isherwood, to proceed to the Norfolk Navy Yard to reassemble the steam propulsion plant on *MERRIMACK*. Also on that day, Confederate forces around Charleston, South Carolina, opened fire on the Union and held Fort Sumter in Charleston Harbor.[95]

Five days later, on 17 April 1861, the Commonwealth of Virginia voted to secede from the Union. Immediately, Confederate President Jefferson Davis saw the Norfolk Navy Yard as a prize he must capture. He ordered two regiments of South Carolina's infantry and two companies from Georgia to report to Confederate Army Major General William Taliaferro with orders to secure the Yard. Isherwood had been successful in reassembling the plant and lighting it off by April 18, 1861. However, Captain McCauley refused to allow *MERRIMACK* to depart and instead ordered her fires secured and her guns to stand by and defend the Yard — a deadly mistake.

The Secretary of the Navy was appalled when he learned this. He ordered a Captain Paulding to immediately relieve Captain McCauley, but he arrived too late to save the Yard. Captain McCauley had ordered the ships in the yard scuttled, including *MERRIMACK*.

Captain Paulding ordered the yard, ships, and Loammi Baldwin's stone dry dock destroyed. Among the ships destroyed were the largest in the United States Navy inventory.

> "The career of the *USS PENNSYLVANIA* [120-gun ship-of-the-line] lacked luster. It spent many years tied up in the Norfolk, Va., Navy Yard and was scuttled in 1861 to avoid Confederate capture during the Civil War."[96]

The *USS DELAWARE* was also doomed, as she was set ablaze — a great tragedy, since this 74-gun ship-of-the-line was given a death sentence, as was the dry dock she made history in 28 years earlier. This fire was one of the primary reasons there are no surviving ships-of-the-line surviving today. A duplicate of the bowsprit of the *DELAWARE* is the figure that now stands facing the United States Naval Academy Bancroft Hall. It is the figure of Tecumseh, the Midshipman "God of 2.0."

It was to be another 48 years before another ship, the *USS DELAWARE, (BB 28*), this time a 20,000 ton battleship, was to be launched in April 1910 at the Newport News Shipbuilding and Drydock Company shipyard. This was almost the exact site of the historic battle between the *MONITOR* and the *MERRIMACK*.

The most significant military facility that Captain Paulding knew had to be destroyed was of course Loammi Baldwin's stone dry dock. Approximately 50 men placed twenty barrels of black powder in the dry dock's hydraulic system.[97] There are conflicting reports as to what exactly happened next.

One account states:
"Commander John Rodgers and Army Captain H. G. Wright were charged with the destruction of the Stone Dry dock. They placed a ton of black powder in the dry dock. Four slow match fuses were set in place. Aboard the *USS CUMBERLAND*, Captain Paulding and Captain McCauley waited for the massive explosion that would signal the destruction of the dry dock. It never came. Confederate Lieutenant Charles F. W. Spottswood is credited with flooding the dry dock and saving it."[98]

Another account states:
"There were thirty barrels of gun powder in [the dry dock]. A powder train led from them to the outside of the dock. A Union petty officer had been assigned to light the slow match that would ignite the powder train. He had been stationed at the Gosport Yard for many months and made friends with many people in the town. He had visited their homes and shared cooked meals in houses across the street from the Yard, a scant 60 yards from the dry dock. As he stood in the dark waiting the signal to light the match, he envisioned the explosion that would send great hunks of

granite flying through the air to crash on the roofs of people who had befriended him. The signal came. He lit the slow match – so that, if questioned, he could say that he had. He then threw it in the river and ran for his boat."[99]

A third account:
"The dry dock did not escape attention. Twenty-six barrels of powder (a quantity sufficient to have destroyed the dock and every building at the south end of the yard) were found undisturbed in the culvert on its north side, and across the head of the dock ..."[100]

Lieutenant C. F. M. Spottswood of the Confederate Navy, is given credit for finding the explosives and saving the dock by ordering the immediate flooding of the graving dock on April 21, 1861. Thus, Stephen R. Mallory, the Confederate Secretary of the Navy — previously Chairman of the U.S. House Naval Affairs Committee [101] — got a tremendous gift from the Union, the dry dock at Norfolk. This gift resulted in deadly consequences to the Union Navy. By May 30, 1861, the *MERRIMACK* had been raised.

The hulk was placed in the saved dry dock and was converted into an ironclad ram. Figure (31) is a rendering of what *MERRIMACK* looked like in the Stone Dry dock after she had been converted into the *CSS VIRGINIA*. This figure also shows a combination of spur shores, which come up from the dock floor, wale shores from the dock altars, and side-blocks which were used to hold the ship upright in the dry dock. The ship undocked in February 1862.

The undocking of the *CSS VIRGINIA*, however, did not go exactly as planned. In fact, it went badly — not surprising with the huge number of structural changes that occurred while the ship was being converted. A 200 ton error was made in the undocking calculations. The Confederate Navy Naval Constructor was Mr. John L. Porter.

"Mr. Porter stated to me that he had accidentally omitted in his calculation some weights which were on the ship, in consequence of which she did not draw as much water when launched as anticipated."[102]

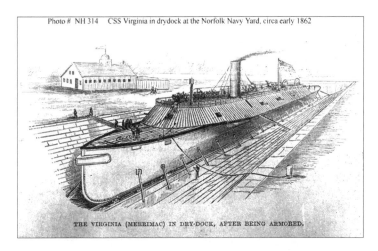

Figure 31 - EX-USS MERRIMACK [CSS VIRGINIA] in dry dock at the Norfolk Navy Yard under the Confederate Navy control May 1861. (Naval Historical Center).

Mr. Porter was unsure enough of the stability of the ship that he added only enough water to just float the ship. Evidently it almost capsized. In attempting to right the ship, the hull caught on the keel blocks. This caused the hull to be damaged by the blocking system. Two hundred tons of ballast had to be added to the bilge of the ship, hull repairs had to be made and machinery removed.[103]

Finally, on February 17, 1862, she was commissioned the *CSS VIRGINIA* under the command of Captain Franklin Buchanan. On March 8, 1862, *CSS VIRGINIA* entered Hampton Roads and immediately rammed and sank the *USS CUMBERLAND* with a resulting great loss of life. Paradoxically, the *CUMBERLAND* had been the escape ship for the maligned Capt. McCauley. So his failure to save the *MERRIMACK* and destroy the dry dock led to the destruction of *CUMBERLAND*. History will unfortunately be forever critical of his decision.

After returning to the Norfolk Navy Yard the night of the 8th, *CSS VIRGINIA* returned to Hampton Roads the next day to participate in one of the most famous naval battles in U.S. Naval history. This was the Battle of the *MONITOR* and the *MERRIMACK*. The epic battle ended with neither vessel seriously damaged.[104] To later avoid capture, May 11, 1862, *CSS VIRGINIA* was sunk by her crew at Craney Island. This is directly across, from what is now the Norfolk Naval Operating Base. She was later raised in May 1876 and was scrapped in Dry Dock Nr. 1. It was her last trip to the Norfolk Navy Yard and the dry dock that had given her renewed life and a naval legacy.[105]

Two eminent naval engineers, John Lenthall and Benjamin F. Isherwood saw this battle as the end to wooden vessels, and an opportunity to build a Navy that would rival any in the world.[106] Pure unarmored sailing ships would never again see a major role in the United States Navy. The age of steel and steam was about to replace the age of oak and sail. The need for dry docks, however, would only increase.

Private shipyards were sprouting up all along the Delaware River waterfront during the Civil War. When the Civil War accelerated the switch from wood to iron warships, private shipyards in Philadelphia adjusted. The Cramp yard became the leading Philadelphia shipyard. This private yard built the hull for the ironclad steam frigate *New Ironsides*, which became a prize warship for the Union Navy.[107]

> "Cramp's son, Charles, wrote that the yard began building 'iron vessels in a comparatively small way' during the war. Cramp's 'became a sort of kindergarten,' he said, 'as most of the workers had to be trained to the work and working appliances had to be designed.'"[108]

Chapter 9

Post War Pause in the East, but Continued Expansion in the West

After the Civil War, the Navy again fell into a state of budgetary neglect. Military spending was low on any political priority list with a country financially and spiritually drained by a war that claimed more human lives than any other in American history. The American people had had enough.

> "After war comes peace, and after the Civil War came the peace which decimated the United States Navy faster than any enemy. ... The Fleet that had numbered almost seven hundred ships in 1866 was cut down to 185 in 1871 and to 139 in 1881. ... By 1885, the Navy had only 90 ships with only 25 operating at sea."[109]

However, it was the Civil War and particularly the disastrous loss of the Norfolk Navy Yard early in the War to the Confederates that convinced Congress of the need for a larger shipyard in Philadelphia.

The Philadelphia Navy Yard was moved to League Island to allow for further expansion and graving dock construction. This was accomplished after Congressional legislation just after the Civil War in 1867, via a financial deal provided by the City of Philadelphia.

> "In 1867, [Congressional legislation passed] to relocate the [Philadelphia] Navy Yard to the very tip of South Philadelphia, at the juncture of the Delaware River and the Schuylkill. The city purchased the so-called League Island site for $320,000 and donated it to the federal government, which, in turn, sold its old yard to the Pennsylvania Railroad for $1 million. The Navy b egan operating there in 1875, and the final move was completed on Jan. 7, 1876."[110]

> "The Philadelphia Navy Yard ... was moved in 1875 from its original site in southeast Philadelphia to the present League

Island site, which had been acquired and developed during the four preceding years."[111]

The Philadelphia Navy Yard was known as the League Island PA Navy Yard. The first graving dock at this location was a timber dry dock. The Philadelphia Navy Yard did utilize its marine railway in 1873 for significant repairs such as the *USS CONSTITUTION*.

However, the Navy as a whole continued to come under political attack in peacetime after the war. Partisan politics ruled the day in the early 1870s and the Navy itself was not without its corruption problems. This also slowed efforts to maintain and upgrade the Navy Yards.

> "In the first two decades after the Civil War, the U.S. Navy was a target of partisan politics. In the elections of 1868 and 1872, the political opponents of Presidents Johnson and Grant attacked the Navy Department for corruption and mismanagement as part of the Democratic Party's larger dispute with the Republicans over Reconstruction policy. Congress repeatedly cut the Navy's appropriations, halting plans that Secretary of the Navy Gideon Welles had laid to maintain a small but technologically efficient fleet with supporting Navy Yards."[112]

As of 1873, there were still only three Navy graving docks. The graving dock at the Mare Island Navy Yard in California had just started excavation the year earlier. In addition, the Navy owned three sectional floating dry docks including two at Philadelphia and one at Mare Island. The Navy also owned one balance type floating dry dock at the Portsmouth Navy Yard.[113]

The East Coast had been traumatized by the Civil War. However, growth in California continued. Commercial interests drove the construction of the first graving dock on the West Coast to become a private sector dry dock. The California Dry Dock Company completed plans for construction of a graving dock at an area just South of San Francisco on the peninsula called Hunters Point. This area later became the San Francisco Bay Naval Shipyard (Hunters Point Division) and was later Hunters Point Naval Shipyard.

Figure (32) is a drawing of this first graving dock at Hunters' Point that was completed in 1868. The construction engineer was

A.W. Von Schmidt, a Civil Engineer for the California Dry Dock Company. This dry dock was originally 500 feet long and later lengthened by 40 more feet. It had a maximum depth of water of 24 feet.

This commercial graving dock provided a repair site for the continued growth of merchant ship traffic in and out of San Francisco. Travel by sea was the primary trade and travel route from the East Coast. Foreign ships frequented the port, also needing the services of a dry dock.

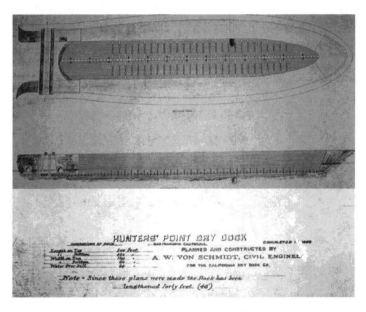

Figure 32 - Drawing of the first dry dock at Hunters' Point near San Francisco 1868. (National Archives)

The U.S. Navy's presence on the West Coast continued to grow, and the larger and heavier steam powered ships required a larger dry dock than the floating dry dock at Mare Island. In 1871, approval for a graving dock at Mare Island was received and engineering work began on the first Navy owned graving dock on the West Coast. Calvin Brown, a civil engineer, designed this stone and concrete dry dock, whose total cost was $2,149,099, about the same order of magnitude as the 1857 estimate for the second dry dock at the Norfolk Navy Yard.

The design of the first U.S. Naval graving dock on the West Coast was heavily influenced by European designs. Engineer Brown had observed the latest design methods at the dockyards in England and France. He used concrete with embedded granite blocks. The dry dock excavation commenced in August 1872. The process was excruciatingly slow using human power extensively. Excavation took almost two years. The pouring of concrete took ten months before the first granite stone was put into place. The granite was transported from quarries in 5-ton blocks.

It was another eleven years before the first ship would be drydocked in this dock. The ship was the old *USS INDEPENDENCE* which was drydocked on October 30, 1886. The graving dock actually did not officially open until February 18, 1891 when the last stone was finally installed.[114] In 1889, Congress appropriated only $80,000 for continued work on the Mare Island granite graving dock; however, the expenditures were only $18,493.99 from March 2, 1889 to July 1, 1889.[115]

The following describes the painstaking and manpower intensive construction process that took a total of 19 years to complete:

> " ... eight different Commandants walked down to inspect that everlasting hole in the ground, in the bottom of which men with picks and shovels labored like ants to remove 83,000 cubic yards of earth, and into which 37,000 cubic yards of concrete and a small mountain of granite disappeared before it was finished."[116]

When completed, the graving dock was 525.9 feet long and 32 feet deep at mean high water. This was about 25 feet longer and 8 feet deeper than the existing commercial graving dock over at Hunters' Point. One of the advantages of this graving dock at Mare Island was its capacity to dry dock large foreign ships as well as the new U.S. Navy ship designs. One of the first ships to be dry docked, even before the official opening, was the French ship *DUQUESNE* on November 2, 1887. At the time, this ship was one of the largest ships in the world.

This construction project brought with it new methods of civil engineering including the production of a massive amounts of concrete at one time, and new pile driving techniques which included the use of gun powder.

> "One the features prominent in the building of dry dock Number One was Engineer Calvin Brown's concrete mixer, a towering wooden contraption of hoppers and chutes in which gravity did the work."[117]

With the completion of the graving dock at Mare Island, the floating dry dock, which had been the only U.S. Navy dry dock on the West Coast for the previous thirty-six years, was sold after it was condemned for further Navy use.[118]

Chapter 10

Post Civil War Doldrums End and Iron Hulls Mean More Drydockings

Navy yards on the East Coast gradually came out of the doldrums in the aftermath of the Civil War. It was not long until a need for a stronger U.S. Navy became apparent yet again. In 1879, navies in South America were expanding rapidly. Chile defeated Peru in the "War of the Pacific." France was showing an interest in building a canal across the Panama Isthmus. The United States Navy was in a state of obsolescence, no match against other navies even in the same hemisphere. Political control changes in the White House and Congress finally quickened a move toward improvements in 1880.

The Navy found itself in need of new ships to counter growing threats in the midst of an industrial revolution where production and use of steel in the United States was emerging as a significant force. The use of iron/steel hulls offered not only a new technological breakthrough to the U.S. Navy, but it offered tremendous Congressional political leverage as well in states that produced steel.

> "By 1881, three factors led to the reconstruction of the Navy and her repair facilities. First, for the first time in six years, the Republicans controlled both houses of Congress and the presidency; second, the domestic situation was quiet and the economy booming; and third, other nations particularly in South America were acquiring naval vessels such that they could easily wipe out the U.S. Navy."[119]

Both the Secretary of the Navy in 1881, William H. Hunt, and the next Secretary of the Navy later in 1881, William E. Chandler urged the design of three new cruisers and a dispatch boat. These would be the first ships built using American-produced steel.

> "Among these vessels were the light cruisers *ATLANTA* and *BOSTON*, and the dispatch boat *DOLPHIN*. Known as the ABCD ships, these first vessels of the new American steel Navy were light and fast, designed for commerce protection

and to show the flag in promising places, such as Asian and African waters."[120]

The momentum had shifted in favor of a new construction for the U.S. Navy. Even when the political party in control of Congress shifted again in 1884, the benefits seen with the jobs created by an emerging Navy were too great to stop. The construction of ships and the growth in the Navy Yards became a political windfall for the politicians. Navy ship construction led to many new jobs in Congressional districts.

A larger Navy was now directly linked to encouraging increased trade abroad and helping establish safe markets for American products by showing the American flag worldwide. More sophisticated ships and navy yards led to technological developments. At this point in American history, there began to be an inexorable partnership between the U.S. Navy and heavy American industry.

> "From this confluence of interrelated interests, the U.S. Navy created a major link in an alliance between government and modern industry..."[121]

With the new steel cruisers *ATLANTA* and *BOSTON* approved and the Navy growing again, larger dry docks at the Navy Yards were an immediate necessity. The use of ironclads by other Navies had led to increased time in dry dock. Ironclads of the French Navy in 1866 spent an average of fifty-five days in dry dock being scraped down.[122] Effective underbody anti-fouling paint systems were still a long way from being effective.

The second dry dock that had been proposed back in 1857 for Norfolk was approved for construction in 1887. Figure (33) is a close up of the drawing and approval document for the proposed location of the second dry dock at the Norfolk Navy Yard. Note the original stone dock (Dry Dock Nr.1) to the left of the proposed location of Dry dock Nr. 2. Figure (34) is a wider view which includes the approval document itself.

The approval document for the location of this second dry dock includes a recommendation from a Board of Officers which included two line officers and two civil engineers. Their recommendation for approval was forwarded to the Chief of the

Bureau of Yards and Docks on April 26, 1887 and approved by him on the next day shown in Figure (34).

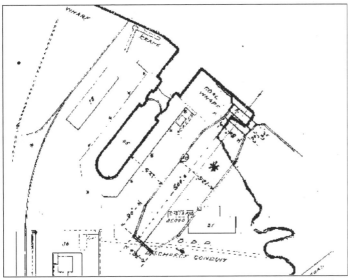

Figure 33 - Close up of the approved site for the location of the second dry dock at Norfolk Navy Yard April 26, 1887.   (National Archives)

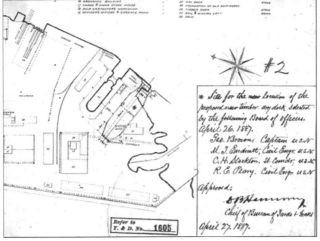

Figure 34 - Wider view of the site drawing and approval statement for the proposed location of the Norfolk Navy Yard. A new timber dry dock was selected by a Naval board of officers on April 26, 1887 and approved by the Chief of Bureau of Yards and Docks on April 27, 1887. (National Archives)

Figure (35) is the legend from the drawing shown in Figures (33, 34, and 36). Figure (36) is the part of the drawing just to the left of Figure (34). Looking closely at these figures one sees a detailed view of what buildings and foundations were present at the Norfolk Navy Yard in 1887. In the upper left corner of Figure (36), locations numbers "1" and "2" are the locations of the foundations of two old shiphouses. On the same figure is the location of the foundation of the old ordnance building. The yard still bore the horrible scars of the burnings of these facilities at the start of the Civil War. These figures provide an excellent example of what went into a Navy yard at the time, including a smithery and stables for the yard's mules, a steam fire engine house, and the all important pay office.

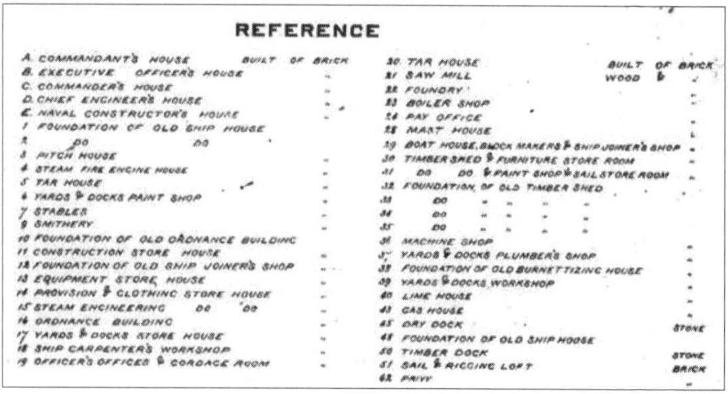

Figure 35 - Reference block on the drawing showing the site for the 2nd dry dock at Norfolk Navy yard approved on April 27, 1887. (National Archives)

This second Norfolk Navy Yard dry dock was named the Simpson Dry Dock. 498'-6" long, it is still in use today. Construction started in November 1887 and was completed September 19, 1889. The dock was first used to dry dock the *YANTIC* on September 19, 1889.[123] Throughout the 1880s, thirty new ships were added to the fleet. The timely completion of this graving dock complimented this growth of the Navy.

The Norfolk Navy Yard now had competition in the Tidewater area for ship repair. Just five months before the Simpson Dry Dock opened at the Norfolk Navy Yard, what was to become the Newport News Shipbuilding and Dry Dock Company (currently

Northrop Grumman Newport News) opened its first dry dock on April 24, 1889 with the docking of the monitor *PURITAN*.

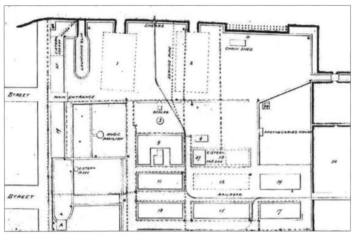

Figure 36 - Rest of the Norfolk Navy Yard as it was on April 27, 1887. (National Archives)

Chapter 11

The Battleship Age and a New Global View

About this time, the preeminent naval theorists, Rear Admiral Stephen B. Luce and Captain Alfred Thayer Mahan, professed the need for a more capable battle fleet. The growing pressure of a growing world-wide steel naval, construction, and steel industry in the United States prompted the Secretary of Navy, Benjamin F. Tracy, to push hard for the construction of battleships. A booming economy, a perceived threat, a cooperative and enthusiastic political environment were all fertile ground for a new U.S. Navy.

> "In December 1889 the new Secretary of the Navy, Benjamin F. Tracy, called for construction of twenty armored battleships – twelve in the Atlantic and eight in the Pacific – that would be combat-ready, even in peacetime. "A war, though defensive in principle," Tracy declared, "may be conducted most effectively by being offensive in operations.".[124]

As result of Secretary Tracy's efforts, on June 30, 1890, Congress passed the Naval Appropriations Act, providing the United States with her first modern battleships. The results were that the U.S. Navy and her Navy Yards grew and grew quickly.

The technological advances brought on by the rapidly advancing Industrial Revolution enabled the construction of complex new warships that rivaled any in the world. At the same time, the Navy Yards started to get away from their purely political practices in personnel hiring and shifted to promotions based on merit. America was starting to expect more from her Navy Yards.[125] This was important as the complexity and time criticalness of the business was increasing.

With the Naval Appropriations Act, construction of Navy Yards and their dry docks proceeded at a quick pace. The second graving dock was completed at the New York Navy Yard in 1890. This dry dock, sized for the new battleships, was 465'6" long and 72 feet wide.[126]

During this period, the use of timber instead of granite for the construction of graving docks grew in popularity before reinforced concrete came of age. The assumptions of timber drydock longevity proved incorrect, as none made entirely of timber construction have survived in the United States today nonetheless, in a report to Congress in 1889 by the Secretary of the Navy, the following statement was made regarding the use of wood vs. granite:

> "The present naval dry docks of the United States are, with three exceptions, made of granite. The exceptions noted are the new docks at New York, League Island [Philadelphia}, and Norfolk. Until recently granite was the sole material used in the construction of such docks, but it has now been demonstrated that dry-docks of wood are almost two-thirds cheaper, and are really more lasting and less costly to repair than those constructed of granite."[127]

In the next 30 years, 16 additional graving docks for the United States Navy would be constructed in 10 different U.S. Naval Shipyards and the Panama Canal Zone. The only period that rivaled this monumental construction effort was World War II.

As Secretary Tracey had envisioned, America's interests in the Pacific grew at a rapid rate. Congress wanted naval stations in the Pacific for the battle fleet that was under construction. A Naval Station was first established at Bremerton, Washington in the Puget Sound in 1891. At the urging of President Harrison in 1891, Congress approved another site for a naval station at Pearl Harbor, Hawaii.[128] These sites soon became locations for Navy Yards and graving docks. With the need for U.S. Naval Stations, came the need for more permanent United States territory in the Pacific. Hawaii was the first location of choice with its obvious strategic importance.

> "On July 27, 1898, Admiral J. N. Miller, U. S. N. Commander in Chief of the United States Naval Force on the Pacific Station, sailed from San Francisco, Cal., for Honolulu, to participate in the ceremonies attending the assumption of sovereignty by the United States over the Hawaiian Islands."[129]

Meanwhile on the East Coast, with the emerging fleet of battleships, there were still not enough dry docks available. The change from wood to steel and the resulting heavier displacements and larger length, width, and draft dimensions made the older floating dry dock at Portsmouth Navy Yard in New Hampshire obsolete. The lack of dry dock capacity in the United States in 1893 forced the cruiser *USS NEW YORK* to go out of the country to Halifax, Nova Scotia to be dry docked.[130]

> "Portsmouth interests cited the advantages of a [dry] dock on the Piscataqua and approval was given for work to start on a new stone dry dock June 4, 1900. The prime contractor was John Pierce Co. of New York for a sum of $1,089,000."[131]

The start of the Spanish American War, sparked by the sinking of the *USS MAINE* in Havana harbor on February 15, 1898, fueled the requirement for more dry docks once again. This war, that ultimately saw battles in both the Pacific and Atlantic, provided the catalyst for the construction of a second graving dock at the Mare Island Yard in California.

> "Washington sent word that a new dry dock would be built at Mare Island. For months, Senator Hilborn [of California] had been doing his best to see that Mare Island got one of the half dozen docks being talked up in Congress. A bigger West Coast dock was certainly needed, with ships growing longer and larger. ... It would be a year [1899] before work commenced on Dry Dock Number Two."[132]

The construction of this second dry dock at Mare Island was not complete until over a decade after it was approved. This 741 foot long dry dock was sized to accommodate Secretary Tracey's battleships.

The Spanish American War in 1898 was the start of a twenty-year expansion period for the United States Navy Fleet. Following the American victory in a war where the U.S. Navy played a prominent role, U.S. Navy Yard growth in construction and repair capacity was extensive, keeping up with the demand for an ever-larger navy.

Figure (37) is a photo of the *USS AILEEN* in dry dock May 17, 1898 at the New York Navy Yard, Brooklyn, New York. She was being converted for naval service. The ship was a 192-ton yacht, built at Chester, Pennsylvania, in 1896 for civilian use. Purchased by the U.S. Navy in April 1898, the *USS AILEEN* served as a coastal defense vessel during the Spanish-American War.[133]

Figure 37 - USS AILEEN in dry dock at the New York Navy Yard, Brooklyn, New York, while being converted for naval service, May 17, 1898. (Naval Historical Center Photograph Photo #: NH 57751)

During this drydocking period the New York Navy Yard added light armor plate to the *USS AILEEN* 's hull amidships to protect her boilers. The wale shores can be seen in the photo extending between the stone altars of the dry dock and the hull of the ship to keep the ship upright in the dry dock.

Figures (38, 39, 40, and 41) are portions of an 1899 drawing that estimated the scope of work and the materials required for the construction of Dry Dock Nr. 2 at the League Island (Philadelphia) Navy Yard. This drawing corresponded to the first specifications for this dry dock and was to be used by bidders to formulate their proposals for the dry dock construction. Ultimately this 744 foot long dry dock was completed in 1908, another dry dock sized to accommodate Secretary Tracy's battleships. The government put a caveat on their estimate requirements, as noted in Figure (38), reminding the bidders that they were assuming all liability for the accuracy of the estimates and must make their own calculations. The Navy attempt to avoid contractors' claims was alive and well even in 1899.

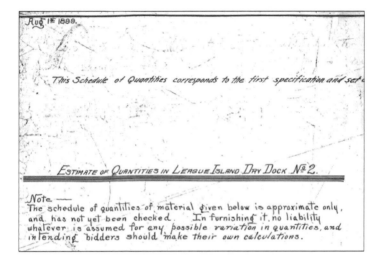

Figure 38 - Notes from the August 1, 1899 Schedule of Quantities drawing for the construction of Dry Dock Nr. 2 at the League Island (Philadelphia) Navy Yard. (National Archives)

As listed in Figure (39), the construction of Dry Dock Nr. 2 at Philadelphia would require 160,000 cubic yards of excavation. The most interesting aspect of this listing of quantities was the requirement for eight electric capstans. Steam was no longer being used in this 1899 design to power the dock-side capstans. Also, over 10,000 piles would be driven consisting of spruce or yellow pine.

Figure (40) lists the materials required for the construction of the caisson for Dry Dock Nr. 2 at Philadelphia. The caisson would have a boiler to power the pump engine and capstans. The caisson would displace 1,219,146 pounds or approximately 600 tons. This included 250 tons of structural steel. Figure (41) lists a 20-ton electric traveling crane as one of the dry dock requirements. Electricity was starting to dominate as the power source of choice for critical dry dock components.

```
DRY DOCK PROPER, shown on GENERAL PLAN, SHEET 143 R, EXCLUSIVE OF CULVERT.
Excavation ___ Exclusive of Dredging in front of Dock (Approximation only) ___ 160,000 cu.yds
Bearing Piles ___ ___ Spruce or Yellow Pine ___ Number of Piles ___ 10,996
     "     at Sills ___ ___ Oak ___ ___ ___ ___ ___ ___ 250
Concrete ___ ___ ___ ___ ___ ___ ___ ___ ___ ___ 9,120 cu.yds
Puddle ___ ___ ___ ___ ___ ___ ___ ___ ___ ___ 8500 "
Grouted Rock in Crib Entrance ___ ___ ___ ___ ___ ___ 756 "
Yellow Pine   Exclusive of Sheet Piling ___ ___ ___ ___ 2,572,000 ft B.M.
         Sheet Piling ___ ___ ___ ___ ___ ___ 1,176,000
White Pine Tongues for Sheet Piling ___ ___ ___ ___ 106,500 ___
Oak (Keel, Bilge Blocks, Slides, Sills &c ___ ___ ___ ___ 161,000 ___
Drift Bolts ___ ___ ___ ___ ___ ___ ___ ___ 156,000 lbs
Screw Bolts & Nuts ___ ___ ___ ___ ___ ___ ___ 47,000
Washers ___ ___ ___ ___ ___ ___ ___ ___ ___ 8,300
Wire Nails ___ ___ ___ ___ ___ ___ ___ ___ 8,100
Galvanized Steel Grating for Culvert ___ ___ ___ ___ 10,000
Composition Metal for Bilge and Keel Block Fittings ___ 100,000
22 Cast Iron Bollards @ 1300# ___ ___ ___ ___ 28,600
31 Cast Iron Bitts
3 Winches
8 Electric Capstans
⅞" Chain ___ ___ ___ ___ ___ ___ ___ ___ 500
18 Wrought Iron Stanchions & Stanchion-sockets

CULVERT
Excavation ___ ___ ___ ___ ___ ___ ___ ___ 2,230 cu.yds
65 Piles
Yellow Pine ___ ___ ___ ___ ___ ___ ___ ___ 12,300 ft B.M.
Concrete ___ ___ ___ ___ ___ ___ ___ ___ 155 cu.yds
Sewer Brick ___ ___ ___ ___ ___ ___ ___ ___ 60,100
Vitrified Brick ___ ___ ___ ___ ___ ___ ___ ___ 14,700
```

Figure 39 - Schedule of Quantities for the Dry Dock Proper and Culvert sections of August 1, 1899 drawing for the construction of Dry Dock Nr. 2 at the League Island (Philadelphia) Navy Yard. (National Archives)

```
CAISSON
                                                                    LBS.
Outside Plating, incl. Liners & Butt Straps ___ ___ ___      186,204
Horizontal      "        "    "                              98,910
Vertical        "     Butt Straps  {55"x55"                  28,222
Keel Channels                      {10"x25"                  27,617
Frames  5"x3½"x13.6" ℔ & 5½"x3½"x17.8"Zs                     51,205
Floor Beams  8"x3½"x19.23" Bulb℔                             27,990
Stanchions: 4"x5"x15.6" Ts                                    7,456
3"x3"x7.2" Ls                                                23,955
4"x3"x9.5" Ls                                                10,572
Misc. Steel Work                                              5,170
              Total ___ ___ ___ ___                        473,041
Rivets, 10% of above                                         47,304
Total Structural Steel                                      520,345
Wrought Iron in Culverts, incl. rivets                       19,323
      "        miscellaneous                                  7,172
Cast Iron                                                     4,950
Composition Metal                                             1,220
Yellow Pine Timber ___ 7100 B.M.                             26,633
Oak and ash                                                  15,858
Glass                                                           285
Rubber                                                        1,350
Cement                                                        2,500
Oakum & Pitch                                                   500
Paint                                                         3,500
2 Capstans                                                    5,600
25 Valves, with stems and wheels ___ ___                     31,550
Boiler & Fittings                                             8,000
Pump, Engine and connections                                  8,760
Concrete Ballast  160 cu.yds @ 3510                         561,600
              Total Weight of Caisson
```

Figure 40 - Schedule of Quantities for the Caisson section of the August 1, 1899 drawing for the construction of Dry Dock Nr. 2 at the League Island (Philadelphia) Navy Yard. (National Archives)

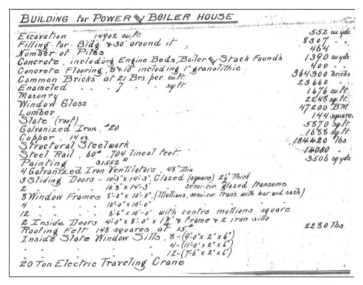

Figure 41 - Schedule of Quantities for the Power and Boiler House section of the August 1, 1899 drawing for the construction of Dry Dock Nr. 2 at the League Island (Philadelphia) Navy Yard. (National Archives)

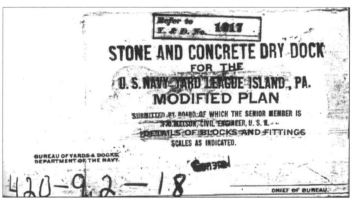

Figure 42 - Title Block for the Details of the Blocks and Fittings for Dry Dock Nr. 2 at the League Island (Philadelphia) Navy Yard. (National Archives)

Figure (42) is the Title Block of the drawing that detailed the side blocks and fittings for Dry Dock Nr. 2 at the League Island (Philadelphia) U.S. Navy Yard. This drawing was submitted for approval by the Chief of the Bureau of Yards and Docks by a Navy Board where the Senior Member was F.O. Maxson, Civil

Engineer, USN. At the time (1899), this dry dock was designated the Stone and Concrete drydock to distinguish it from the Timber Dry Dock (Dry Dock Nr. 1). Timber was losing favor as a construction material for graving docks.

Figure (43) is part of the Dry Dock Nr. 2 at Philadelphia Navy Yard drawing, showing the overall arrangement of the side (or bilge) blocks for Dry Dock Nr. 2 at Philadelphia. There were 68 side blocks in all, 34 on each side of the dry dock. Figures (44 and 45) are close-ups of the side block components. This arrangement was typical of most dry dock side block configurations. This type of mechanism for hauling side blocks in and out is still being used today primarily in floating dry docks.

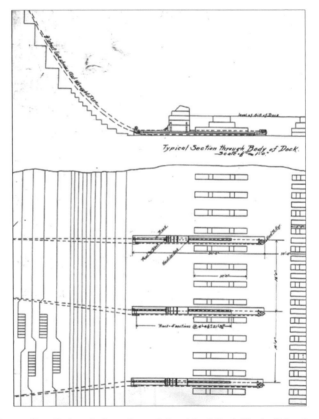

Figure 43 - End and plan view of the side (bilge) block slides for Dry Dock Nr. 2 at the League Island (Philadelphia) Navy Yard. (National Archives)

Basically, the approach was to haul the side blocks in against the hull of a ship once the ship was in the dock and the water in the dock was pumped down to a point where the ship had fully landed on the keel blocks. There still had to be enough water around the ship so the ship would not lose positive stability and so the side block was buoyant enough to make it possible for the side block assembly to slide along the oak slide toward the ship's hull.

In order to operate the side blocks, three pulleys were required. All three were fixed to the 30-foot long oak slide base, two on the outboard end and one on the inboard end of the slide. These pulleys were single sheave pulleys through which passed a 3/8-inch short link galvanized wrought iron chain. The sheaves were made of galvanized cast iron. The outboard pulleys are shown in Figure (44), and the inboard pulley, is shown in Figure (45). The outboard pulleys were placed in a vertical position on the slide and the inboard pulley was placed in a horizontal position.

Two chains were required. One chain, called the inhaul chain, started at the inboard end of the side block assembly and proceeded inboard through the horizontal pulley on the inboard end of the oak slide. From there, it went all the way to the outboard end along the side of the oak slide, through the vertical pulley, then up the side of the dry dock. When the ship had fully landed on the blocks, after sufficient water was pumped out of the dry dock, the side blocks were hauled in by pulling on the inhaul chain. The chain was pulled on until the side block was firmly against the ship's hull. A pawl on the outboard end of the side block assembly repeatedly fell into the teeth of the rack track that the side block assembly passed over. This galvanized cast iron rack and the pawl on the slide block assembly prevented this assembly from backing away from the hull of the ship once in place.

The other chain was attached to the outboard end of the side block assembly at the pawl and was led through the pulley on the center of the outboard end of the slide. From there, the chain went up the side of the dry dock to top where it could be operated during the docking evolutions. This chain was used to pull the side blocks away from the ship's hull when the ship was leaving the dry dock. When the chain was pulled, it pulled the pawl up from the rack releasing it, and thus, allowing the slide block assembly to be pulled away from the ship's hull.

This was done when there was sufficient water in the dry dock to provide the ship enough buoyancy to stay upright without the side blocks in place.

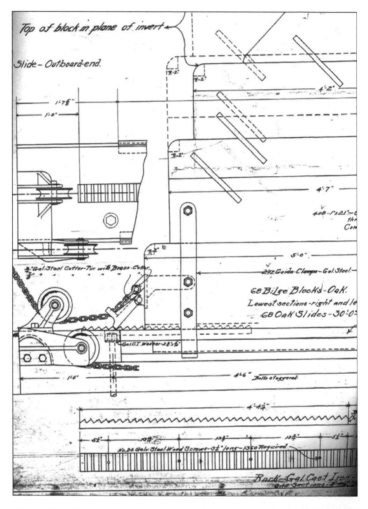

Figure 44 - Close-up of outboard end of a typical side (bilge) block slide for Dry Dock Nr. 2 at the League Island (Philadelphia) Navy Yard. (National Archives)

Figures (46 and 47) are part of another 1900 drawing of Dry Dock Nr. 2 at Philadelphia. Figure (47) is part of a cross section view of the dry dock's wall and culvert. Surface areas of the dry dock wall were covered with a 1-inch granolithic surface. The flooding culvert consisted of a 4-layer brick arch built near the entrance to the dry dock. Further in the culvert, a single layer of vitrified brick (brick containing glass) was used. 9120 cubic yards of concrete were required to build this dry dock. Concrete had come of age in graving dock construction.

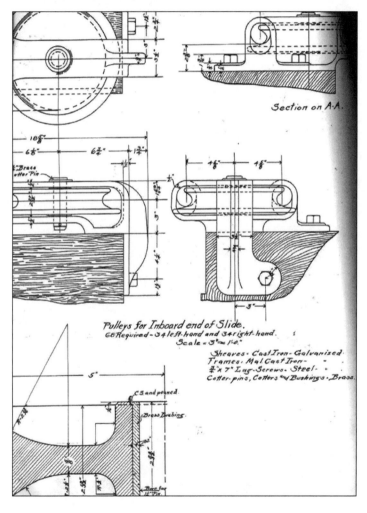

Figure 45 - Close-up of inboard end of a typical side (bilge) block slide pulley for Dry Dock Nr. 2 at the League Island (Philadelphia) Navy Yard. (National Archives)

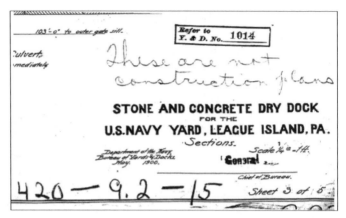

Figure 46 - Bureau of Yards and Docks drawing legend for the Stone and Concrete Dry dock at the League Island (Philadelphia), PA Navy Yard May 1900. (National Archives)

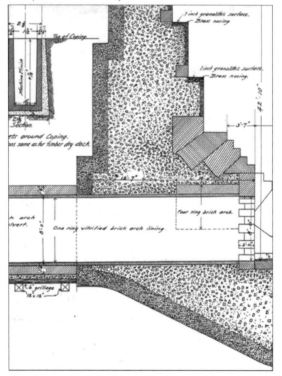

Figure 47 - Bureau of Yards and Docks cross-section drawing for the Stone and Concrete Dry dock at the League Island (Philadelphia), PA Navy Yard May 1900. (National Archives)

Sir Winston Churchill wrote the following about the United States' new colonial role post the Spanish American War:

> "The United States, though not yet abandoning isolation, henceforth became less preoccupied by home affairs. They began to play an important role in the international scene."[134]

Obviously, the Navy was to be a key player in this new role for the United States. With a larger Navy came the immediate need for more graving docks. The first graving dock at Puget Sound (Bremerton, Washington) is shown in Figure (48). This dock was used to drydock the *USS IOWA (BB 4)* in 1900. Puget Sound officially became a Navy Yard in 1901.

Figure 48 - The Battleship USS IOWA entering Dry Dock Nr. 1 in 1900 at Puget Sound Navy Yard. (U.S. Navy Photo).

The next Navy Yard that would be established for the United States Navy was at Charleston, South Carolina, also in 1901. The construction of additional dry docks at Norfolk was lockstep with the commissioning of larger warships. The next Norfolk Navy Yard dry dock construction (Dry Dock Nr. 3) commenced on November 30, 1903 and was completed in 1908.

At the Portsmouth Navy Yard in New Hampshire, the first graving dock was completed in 1904, although it was not accepted until 1906. The following describes the construction process of this dry dock.

"A total of 166,000 cubic yards of rock were blasted away using steam drills and dynamite. After the site was excavated, some 18,000 cubic yards of Portland cement concrete were poured as a base for the granite. The floor and walls of the basin were composed of 20,500 cubic yards of granite ... the 750-foot dock was completed [in 1904] as one of the world's largest and finest."[135]

It was this same year (1904) that the United States started construction of the Panama Canal, employing much of the same technology used in dry dock construction. The Panama Canal was completed in 1914. One of the primary reasons for the construction of this enormous canal was to enable the U.S. Navy to quickly move the new battleships being constructed from one ocean and coast to another. Six battleships were commissioned in 1906 and four more in 1907.

Chapter 12

Global Reach and the Need for a Forward Deployed Floating Dry Dock

The Great White Fleet that included 16 battleships made its "round the world" voyage in 1907-1909. With U.S. Navy vessels now sailing in the Western Pacific in large numbers, the need for a forward deployed maintenance facility became apparent.

> "The Navy in 1903 as a result of Admiral Evan's exercise, directed (the opening) of the former Spanish Naval Station at Olongapo as a U.S. Naval Base. The base (was) to be used as an ammunition and coaling substation of the Cavite Naval Yard in Manila Bay (and included) the addition of the floating dry dock Dewey towed to Subic from the United States in 1905 ...."[136]

Indeed, in 1906, the United States Navy not only sent the Great White Fleet battleships around the world, they also projected power by towing the first U.S. Navy floating dry dock half way around the world. This floating dry dock, named the *DEWEY*, was built at Sparrows Point, Maryland near Baltimore under the direction of Rear Admiral Mordecai T. Endicott, the father of the Navy's Civil Engineering Corp.

> "[Rear Admiral Mordecai T. Endicott, a graduate of Rensselaer Polytechnic Institute in 1868] was commissioned as a civil engineer in the U.S. Navy in 1874 and by 1890 was posted to Washington, D.C., and given control of all civil engineering projects. The Navy yards were undergoing extensive modernization and Endicott introduced electronic appliances and steel and concrete dry docks. He was the builder of the floating dry dock *Dewey*, at the time the largest built. Immediately before the Spanish-American War, President McKinley broke precedent and appointed Endicott Chief of the Bureau of Yards and Docks, a post always before held by an officer of the line."[137]

The *DEWEY* was designated as YFD-1 or Yard Floating Drydock. A series of tests took place near Solomons in the Chesapeake Bay, where there was deep enough water for the necessary submergence tests. The *DEWEY* completed in 1905. The cruiser *USS COLORADO* and the battleship *USS IOWA* were used for these submergence tests. It was common at the time to use actual capital ships to test floating dry docks. Figure (49) shows the *USS ILLINOIS* in a floating dry dock at New Orleans January 6, 1902, conducting the dock's load and operational test. Boilers in the floating dry dock's wing walls provided the steam engines for the pumping power of the dock.

Figure 49 - USS ILLINOIS (BB 7) in floating dry dock during the dock's load and operational test on January 6, 1902. (Naval Historical Center).

The story of the *DEWEY (YFD-1)* is an inspiring story of sound engineering, yet a fight against the ravages of the both the sea and war. She was to eventually lose her fight to survive at the start of World War II.

> "In 1905, ... the Navy selected the mouth of the Patuxent as the best site in the tidewater to test the famous *Dewey* floating dry dock, recently constructed at Sparrow's Point, Baltimore, and completed at Solomons by the Maryland Steel Company. This mammoth, 500x100 foot long, 16,000-ton vessel needed deep water for its test and the waters off Solomons fit the bill. In the final test for the craft the cruiser *USS Colorado* was dry-docked, followed by the battleship *USS Iowa*. In both cases, the *Dewey* passed with flying colors."[138]

Starting three days after Christmas, December 28, 1905, the *DEWEY's* tow to the Philippines commenced. She was towed across the Atlantic, through the Mediterranean and Suez Canal, and across the Indian Ocean to the Philippines.[139] This was an unprecedented achievement for the time. This was the start of the United States Navy's organic overseas repair capability for underwater hulls.

The tow of the *DEWEY* from the Patuxent River in the Chesapeake Bay, to the Olongapo Naval Station, Philippine Islands took six and a half months and she arrived on July 10, 1906. The voyage was arduous for all involved. Four ships were assigned to this long history making tow for the United States Navy. The ships were the naval supply ship *GLACIER*, colliers *BRUTUS* and *CAESER*, and the naval tug *POTOMAC*. This 195-day expedition took the lives of at least two crewmembers with many others severely injured with the tow being lost many times. They averaged 87 miles a day and burned 12,000 tons of coal at a cost of $58,000.[140]

The *DEWEY (YFD-1)* had considerable lifting power in proportion to her length. It was suitable for naval purposes due to its short and broad dimensions. The dry dock was 500 feet long, 135 feet wide and 18 feet deep, displacing 12,000 tons with a draft of approximately 8 feet. The engineers who designed *DEWEY* were Mr. Sven Anderson and Mr. Cunningham of the Maryland Steel Company.[141]

Figures (50) and (51) show the *USS CLEVELAND* drydocked in the DEWEY at Olongapo on January 14, 1908. For this drydocking, a combination of hauled side blocks and wale shores were used to keep *CLEVELAND* upright.

Figure 50 - USS Cleveland (Cruiser # 19) In the DEWEY dry dock, Olongapo Naval Station, Philippine Islands, January 14, 1908. (Naval Historical Center).

Figure 51 - Stern view of USS Cleveland (Cruiser # 19) in the DEWEY dry dock, Olongapo Naval Station, Philippine Islands, January 14, 1908. (Naval Historical Center).

Chapter 13

Graving Docks on the West Coast and Hawaii Become the Priority

With the advent of major Naval action in the Philippines during the Spanish American War in 1898, graving dock construction became a priority on the West Coast and Hawaii. Figure (52) is a 1907 plan of the dry docks at Hunter's Point near San Francisco, and shows a considerable number of features of the 1907 graving dock design. Illustrated in this figure are two dry docks, Nrs. 1 and 2, at the Hunters Point Yard. Located between the two dry docks is an engine room that contained three 38" centrifugal pumps powered via a rope drive powered by Allis and Corliss horizontal engines. These engines supplied a total of 1000 HP to the pumps. Supplying steam to these engines were 1275 HP B&W (Babcock and Wilcox) boilers. There is one suction line coming from each of the dry docks to the engine room with one discharge tunnel from the pump house to the San Francisco Bay.

Appearing in Figure (52), along the sides of the Dry Dock Nr. 2, are several steam powered capstans used for exact ship positioning over the dry dock blocks. This was an upgrade compared to Dry Dock Nr. 1 which was built 40 years earlier. Dry Dock Nr 2 at the Hunter Point Yard was 750' long and 122' wide. Both dry docks at this point used caissons instead of gates to hold the water out of the dry dock.

Caissons were more easily repaired compared to the gates used in earlier dry dock designs. To remove the caisson, the dry dock had to be fully flooded until the water level in the dry dock was equalized with the current tide level. The caisson was then deballasted via pumps and then moved out of the dry dock sill using tugboats and lines. The caisson could be dry docked itself for repairs. It was occasionally necessary to repair the gasket seal where the caisson came in contact with the dry dock sill area. Some caissons had such seals on both sides of the caisson. The side of the caisson used against the sill would be alternated.

Figure (53) is the title block from the Hunter's Point plan. What had been the California Dry Dock Company was now the San

Francisco Dry Dock Company, and this shipyard later became the Hunter's Point Navy Yard. The heavy silting being experienced at the nearby Mare Island Navy Yard necessitated the use of this yard by the Navy.

> "Partial relief of unsatisfactory conditions at Mare Island, occasioned by heavy silting of Mare Island Strait, had also been achieved by use of privately owned facilities at Hunters Point, on San Francisco Bay and within the city limits of San Francisco."[142]

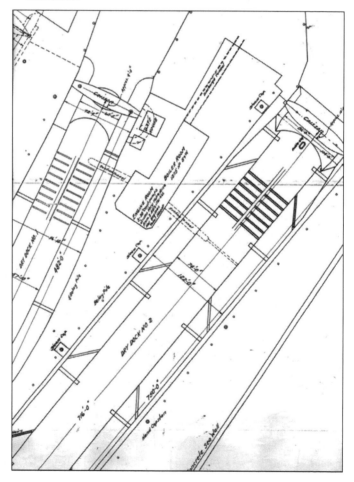

Figure 52 - Plan of dry docks at Hunters Point (San Francisco Dry Dock Company) near San Francisco, California 1907. (National Archives)

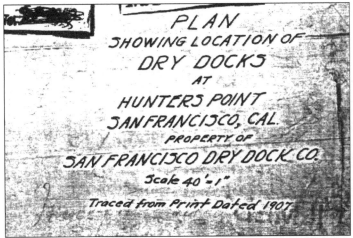

Figure 53 - Title section of drawing of dry docks at Hunters Point (San Francisco Dry Dock Company) near San Francisco, California 1907. (National Archives)

Shortly after the completion of a major drydocking facility, the U.S. Navy came calling. The new commercial dry dock at Hunters Point was to contribute to the sailing of the Great White Fleet. From May 9th to June 29th, 1908 twelve battleships of the Great White Fleet were drydocked in the San Francisco Dry Dock Company's large dry dock: *USS MISSOURI, USS ALABAMA, USS MAINE, USS OHIO, USS LOUISIANA, USS CONNECTICUT, USS MINNESOTA, USS VERMONT, USS KANSAS, USS CALIFORNIA, USS TENNESSEE*, and the *USS WASHINGTON*.[143] The following is a quote from Assistant Naval Constructor L. B. McBride, on December 2, 1908, describing the commercial dry dock at Hunter's Point:

> "The dock here used is an excellent one, containing many good features and with a plant designed for the greatest economy in operation. ... The real bottom of the dock is cement, but on this is laid a 4-inch wood floor, which is of a great convenience enabling the dogging down of blocks or shores at any point whatever.... The pumping plant consists of six Babcock & Wilcox oil-burning boilers; one small auxiliary boiler ... three large horizontal Corliss engines installed on the ground level, three 40,000-gallon centrifugal pumps installed in a pit of such depth that they pick up the water in the docks when it is about 5 feet from the bottom,

and one small reciprocating drain pump also in the pit. The pumps are driven by rope belting from the engines."[144]

New shipyards opened with their associated dry docks allowing the fleet to strategically, as well as politically, spread out. A larger fleet required additional political support. It also presented a legitimate strategic benefit by not concentrating this larger Navy in any one area.

In 1907, the first graving dock in the South opened. This was the 622 foot long Dry Dock Nr. 1 at the Charleston Navy Yard, Charleston, South Carolina.

In May of 1908, the U.S. Naval Shipyard at Pearl Harbor, Hawaii was established. Congress authorized $2,000,000 to be expended on the construction of a graving dock, but that amount was insufficient. After considerable controversy about the design affordability, Congress authorized another $1,178,621.21. Construction of this 1001-foot long graving dock started on September 21, 1909. It would take another 10 years to complete.[145]

Meanwhile, in Europe, naval expansion was on the move, adding to this political pressure for continued American naval ship construction.

> "On November 3 [1909], with [Winston Churchill's] German visit much in mind, Churchill set down for the Cabinet his thoughts on German naval intentions. There were 'practically no checks upon German naval expansion', he wrote, 'except those imposed by the difficulties of getting money'".[146]

> "The dispute rumbled on for the next four months, ... as Churchill and Lloyd George had wished, that only four new battleships should be laid down in 1909. But he appeased the 'big navy' supporters by agreeing that a further four should be laid down in 1910."[147]

Amidst this increasing naval construction interest, existing U.S. Navy Yard dry dock capacity continued to grow. The first ship drydocked in a new 741 foot long graving dock (Dry Dock Nr.2) at Mare Island on March 14, 1910, was the *USS SOUTH DAKOTA*.[148] Even though Dry Dock Nr. 3 at the

Norfolk Navy Yard was just completed in 1908, this graving dock was extended during the period 1910 to 1911 to a new length of 723' 6."[149] This was required to accommodate the new battleships, including the *USS MICHIGAN (BB 27)*, the first American dreadnaught. *MICHIGAN* was commissioned on January 4, 1910.[150]

The second graving dock at the Puget Sound Navy Yard was completed in 1912. It is shown under construction in Figure (54). This graving dock was 867 feet long and could accommodate a ship 112'5" wide.

Figure 54 - Puget Sound Navy Yard Dry Dock 2 under construction. Construction began in 1909 and concluded in 1912. (U.S. Navy photo)

Progress in 1913 on the first graving dock under construction on the Islands of Hawaii hit a snag that even previous naval visionaries such as Rear Admiral Luce and Captain Mahan could not have imagined. The problem was directly related to a native religious custom and superstition. A catastrophic cave-in of the dry dock on February 17, 1913 led to immediate concern by the workers, who believed that the Hawaiian God Kaahupahau, the shark Goddess, was opposing the project.

The actual cause of the failure was determined to be an inadequate dry dock wall thickness. The local workers did not accept this explanation. The help of a Hawaiian priestess was finally solicited, and only after she had properly blessed the dry dock was the issue resolved. The following excerpt describes the event:

> "A worker on the dry dock named David Kanakeawe Richards became seriously disturbed by the murmurings of his fellow-laborers. These continued even after work was resumed in 1915. ... He visited a local kahuna, a priestess, who told him what should be done. The man sprinkled wood and ashes over the dry dock as she instructed him, chanting Hawaiian phrases all the while. The kahuna herself came by a few days later to add her powers of invocation to those of Mr. Richards. After she had blessed the dry dock enterprise and appeased Kaahupahau she told Navy officials they would have no further trouble ... [and] neither that dry dock nor any of the other three built since have collapsed."[151]

The "blessed" Dry Dock Nr. 1 even survived the Japanese attack of Pearl Harbor, although the ships in the dry dock did not fare so well. By 1916, much progress had been accomplished at the Pearl Navy Yard. An ammunition depot and U.S. Naval Hospital had been completed. The first section of Dry Dock Nr. 1 was in place. The investment by Congress in the Pearl Navy Yard to date (1916) was over 10 million dollars.[152]

Chapter 14

Panama Canal Completes, World War I Starts and Dry Dock Construction Surges

Work on graving docks for the United States Navy continued in earnest along the Atlantic Coast and the Pacific. The Panama Canal itself was used as a dry dock for U.S. Naval vessels four months prior to the Canal becoming fully operational. On March 9, 1914, five U.S. Navy submarines (C-1, C-2, C-3, C-4 and C-5) along with the canal ladder dredge, *COROZAL*, were drydocked for repairs in the upper east chamber of the Gatun Locks. They were successfully undocked on April 11, 1914. The Canal itself was fully operational in August 1914.[153]

> "The use of a lock chamber for drydocking proved satisfactory. Keel blocks were secured to the lock floor by tying to cross beams in the athwartship culverts, which gave sufficiently rigid blocking ..."[154]

Just two years, after the completion of the Panama Canal, the largest graving dock built up to that time was completed at Balboa, Canal Zone. This graving dock was 1076 feet long. Having this huge dry dock at the Canal Zone provided an essential ship repair capacity at this most strategic site for the United States Navy. The graving dock was large enough to accommodate the largest U.S. warships at the time.

Also in 1916, work on a new graving dock (Dry Dock Nr. 4) at Norfolk continued. The drawing for this dry dock was approved on September 11, 1916, as shown in the drawing title block in Figure (55). Figure (56) is part of a construction drawing for this dry dock showing a cross section of the sluice gate chamber.

The sluice gates are used to control the flooding of the graving dock. When these gates are opened, water is let into the dry dock and directed to the dry dock floor, via flooding tunnels.

Work on the graving docks in 1916 was being driven by the new warship designs coming off the ways. In 1916, the first oil fired super dreadnaught battleships *NEVADA, OKLAHOMA, PENNSYLVANIA,* and *ARIZONA* were commissioned.[155] Construction of Dry Dock Nr. 4 at Norfolk Naval started on 8 January 1917. However, only three months later, the United States entered into World War I in Europe. By the end of 1917 (December 7, 1917), five U.S. Navy battleships had been sent to Northern Europe to help England.

"On, 7 December 1917, five U.S. Navy dreadnoughts comprising Battleship Division 9 – the *DELWARE (BB 28), FLORIDA (BB 35), NEW YORK (BB34), TEXAS (BB 35),* and *WYOMING (BB 32)* – Rear Admiral Hugh Rodman, commanding, arrive at Scapa Flow in the Orkneys to reinforce the British Grand Fleet, in which they become the Sixth Battle Squadron."[156]

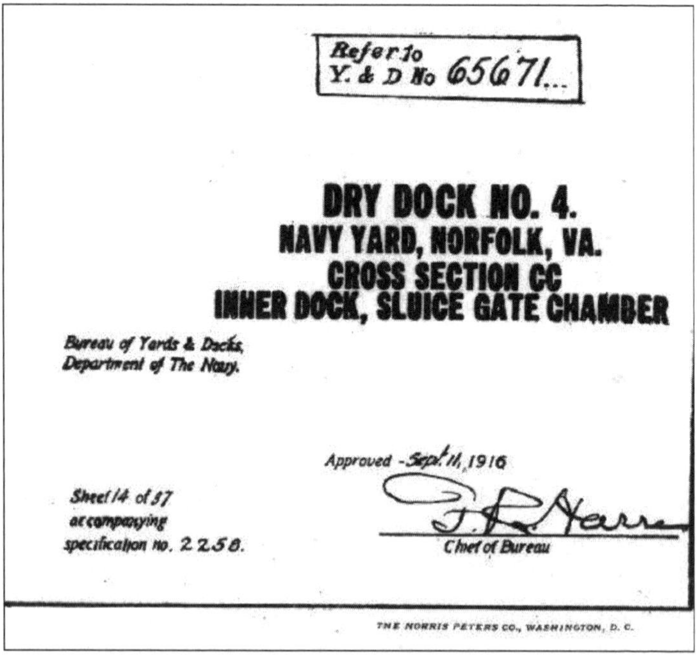

Figure 55 - Title section of Bureau of Yards and Docks construction drawing of the Norfolk Navy Yard Sluice Gate chamber for Dry Dock Nr. 4 approved September 11, 1916. (National Archives)

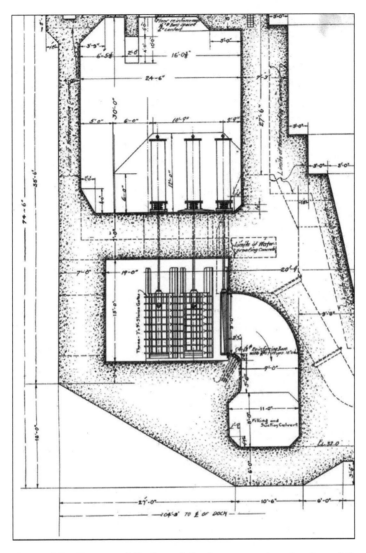

Figure 56 - Bureau of Yards and Docks construction drawing of the Norfolk Navy Yard Dry Dock Nr. 4. Sluice Gate chamber approved September 11, 1916. (National Archives)

Wartime requirements for new construction of ships quickly outpaced the capacity of public yards. Shipyards sprang up quickly and employment exploded. However, the life of these private yards was sometimes brief as their workload was tied only to a wartime footing. Capital investment at these private yards was the minimum possible for ship construction.

> "Wartime meant brisk business for the shipyards, and peacetime often meant decline. Such was the demand for ships in World War I that the nation's largest shipyard was built from scratch in 10 months on Philadelphia's Hog Island. It laid its first keel on February 12, 1918. The yard employed 35,000 men and women whose fast-food luncheon sandwiches took their name from the island. Hoagies, as they were called, are still around, but the yard isn't. It closed in January 1921 after delivering 122 ships. Its site is now occupied by Philadelphia International Airport runways."[157]

Meanwhile, battleship construction continued, as did dry dock construction. However, World War I ended on what is now celebrated as Veterans Day in November of 1918.

> "December 18 [1917] the battleship *MISSISSIPPI (BB 41)* is commissioned. ... May 20 [1918] the battleship *NEW MEXICO (BB 40)* is commissioned."[158]

> "... the war [came to an] abrupt and unforeseen end in November 1918 ..."[159]

Dry Dock Nr. 4 at the Norfolk Navy Yard opened on April 1, 1919, four and a half months after the end to World War I. This mammoth 1011-foot long dry dock, although completed in just over two years, was not available during the War effort. Once again, dry dock construction lagged behind rapidly changing world events.

The first drydocking that occurred in Dry Dock Nr. 4 at the Norfolk Navy Yard is shown in Figure (57), which shows the battleship *USS WISCONSIN* on May 5, 1919. The *USS NEVADA* is also shown to the left of Figure (57) in Dry Dock Nr. 3. *NEVADA* was the first oil-fired battleship of the U.S. Navy. Steam can be seen being expelled from *NEVADA* and her signal flags are flying, as she is either just entering or ready to leave the graving dock with her boilers fired. Also of note, in this photo a mule is barely seen in the lower left corner next to a cart. Beasts of burden were still used in the U.S. Navy Yards well into the 20th century. The shipyards had stables and blacksmiths.[160]

Figure 57 - First drydocking in Dry Dock Nr. 4 Norfolk Navy Yard on May 5, 1919. Ship is the USS WISCONSIN. The USS NEVADA is in Dry Dock Nr. 3 to the left in this photo. (National Archives)

Dry Dock Nr. 4 was and still is a huge graving dock. This graving dock was originally designed to have a sill half way down the dock so two ships could be simultaneously drydocked, and the one closest to the dry dock entrance could be removed without having to flood the other end of the dry dock. A caisson would be put in the sill between the two sections of the dock. Sluice gates prevented water from flooding the inbourd end of the dock.

Figure (58) is a closer view of Dry Dock Nr. 4 that shows the blocking system used in this newly opened graving dock. The side blocks could be hauled in and out.

Dry Dock Nr. 4 is 1011 feet long. The *WISCONSIN* shown in Figure (58) is sitting in the furthest position in the graving dock, and there is enough room left in the dock for another ship of similar size.

Additional graving dock construction proceeded at Pearl Harbor, Hawaii; Bremerton, Washington; Philadelphia, Pennsylvania; and Boston, Massachusetts. The first graving dock (Dry Dock Nr. 1) in Hawaii (the "blessed" dock) was finally completed on August 21, 1919. Figure (59) shows the opening ceremony of this graving dock. Mrs. Josephus Daniels, wife of the Secretary of the Navy, officially opened it. My grandfather, Commander Joseph F.

Daniels, USN, was a Naval Aide to the Secretary of the Navy close to this time period.

"... Mrs. Daniels, wearing a hat that could pass for a small shade tree, pressed a button that started flooding the dock... while simultaneously causing an American flag to be run up a mast on the dry dock's caisson."[161]

Figure 58 - Close-up of USS WISCONSIN in Dry Dock Nr. 4 Norfolk Naval Shipyard May 5, 1919. (National Archives)

Figure 59 - Opening ceremony of Dry Dock Nr. 1 at Pearl Harbor Navy Yard. (U.S. Navy Photo)

The first ship to be drydocked at Pearl Harbor entered the drydock on October 1, 1919. The battleships now had a mid Pacific repair site, a fact, twenty-two years later, that heavily contributed to reconstituting the Navy after the attack on Pearl Harbor and set the logistical stage for the rest of World War II in the Pacific.

Dry Dock Nr. 3 at Puget Sound Naval Shipyard at Bremerton, Washington was also completed in 1919. This dry dock, like Dry Dock Nr. 4 at Norfolk, was long enough (926'8") to also have a sill for a caisson at the halfway point [489'7"] from the end of the dry dock.[162] The concept of the design was to increase the dry dock flexibility and efficiency. This one graving dock could drydock two or more ships at the same time. However, if repairs to the ships at the caisson end of the dry dock were completed first, these ships could be undocked without affecting the other ships. The caisson in between would, similar to Dry Dock Nr. 4 configuration at Norfolk, keep the inward ships dry, eliminating the necessity to float them off the blocks, stopping all underbody work.

Figure (60) is part of a 1919 status of construction blueprint for Dry Dock Nr. 3 at the Philadelphia Navy Yard. It shows the dates each section of this 1011-foot long dry dock was completed. This dry dock would be the third largest graving dock owned by the U.S. Navy at the time when completed. With the completion of Dry Dock Nr. 3, employment soared at the yard.

"The Philadelphia Naval Shipyard outfitted ships but built none at its League Island location, until an 11,250-ton transport was launched in 1917. Then piers were added, a huge dry dock was built, and employment soared from 2,500 in 1916 to 12,000 in 1919."[163]

The use of floating dry docks continued to grow as well, throughout the Navy. Since floating dry docks were still powered by steam boilers, the United States Navy had strict rules governing their operation. According to the 1920 version of United States Navy Regulations:

> "No floating dry dock shall be submerged below the main or working deck without sufficient steam pressure in the boilers to enable the dock to be immediately pumped up. Floating dry dock boilers must maintain enough steam while a ship is in dry dock to pump out ballast tanks."[164]

This requirement was probably learned the hard way during early deployments of these floating dry docks. The regulation would require the boilers to be operating the entire time a ship was in the dry dock. If the boilers were secured for some reason, and the dry dock started to take on water, catastrophic damage could happen to a ship in the dry dock that had part of its hull under repair submerged and not yet water tight.

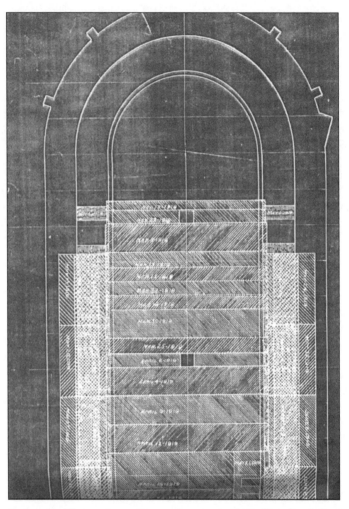

Figure 60 - Status of construction drawing in 1919 of Dry Dock Nr. 3 at the Philadelphia Navy Yard. Dates indicate when sections were completed. (National Archives)

Unlike graving docks, with floating dry docks, stability of the entire ship and dry dock system is a constant concern. There is a point of minimum stability for the entire system. This occurs when water first covers the pontoon deck of the floating dry dock when ballasting down. Stability is again increased, when the dock is ballasted down to a point where part of the ships hull starts to be covered. During this period of minimum stability, fast changes in list (or heel) can occur without warning, potentially damaging equipment, the dry dock, and the ship, let alone personnel. Another major concern is the pumping plan of the dry dock during ballasting and deballasting, taking into account the load distribution of the ship. If the dry dock's ballast tanks are not filled or pumped out to the exact right levels, the structural bending limits of the dry dock could be exceeded and the dry dock could suffer a catastrophic failure.

Completion of the longest graving dock constructed, to date in the United States occurred in Boston in 1920. This dry dock (Dry Dock Nr. 3) is shown here in Figure (61) and was the graving dock at the South Boston Annex of the Boston Navy Yard. Figure (62) is a photo of the *USS DELAWARE* looking aft in Dry Dock Nr. 3 at South Boston 30 January 1924. This graving dock is 1152 feet long, 119 feet wide with a depth of 51 feet. The *DELAWARE* was being scrapped as part of the reductions of capital ships as required by the Washington Naval Conference in 1922. This graving dock still exists today and can be seen when flying out of Logan Airport over the City of Boston. The dock was recently used in November 1998 to drydock the historic World War II battleship *USS MASSACHUSETTS*. Passengers flying into Logan Airport in Boston in January 1999, could see the *USS MASSACHUSETTS* in the dock with her hull shrouded for blasting and painting.

Figure 61 - USS DELAWARE (BB 28) on January 30, 1924 during scrapping at the South Boston Annex, Boston Navy Yard. (Naval Historical Center)

Looking closely at Figure (62), the inhaul and outhaul chains to the side blocks can be seen descending from the top of the graving dock walls along the length of the dock. Figure (62) faces aft at the Number 2 gun turret upon which cutting is occurring. The dry dock's caisson can be seen at the end of this long dry dock. Workers were walking about the deck wearing soft hats popular in the day. Hard hats, were yet to be a required safety standard.

Figure 62 - USS DELAWARE in dry dock at South Boston, January 30, 1924. (National Archives)

Battleship construction, which had been authorized World War I, was not complete until well after the war, and the Washington Naval Conference which commenced 12 November 1921[165] and concluded February 1922 doomed additional battleship construction. This prohibition of capital ship construction was later extended to 1936. Again, post war anti-naval sentiment led to a period in the United States where no graving docks would be completed for another generation, except one 386 ft long graving dock at Cristobal Canal Zone in 1933.

> "The *MARYLAND* – class "super dreadnaught" *USS COLORADO* was authorized in the naval expansion of 1916, laid down at the New York Shipbuilding yard in 1919, and launched in 1921. With her sixteen-inch guns, oil fired

turbine engines, electric power, and twenty-one knot speed, the 600-foot *COLORADO* reflected President Wilson's big navy program that challenged British naval superiority."[166]

"In the 1920's the Washington Naval Conference agreements on arms limitations, reached in 1922, and a new wave of anti-navalism would prove a disappointing period for those whose vision of a powerful America rested upon naval omnipotence."[167]

Dry Dock Nr. 3 at Philadelphia was completed in 1921. A plan view of the Delaware River end of the dock is shown in Figure (63).

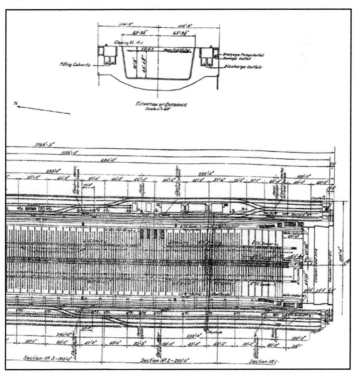

Figure 63 - Part of drawing of Dry Dock Nr. 3 (caisson end) Philadelphia Navy Yard. (U.S. Navy, Bureau of Yards and Docks U.S. Navy)

Figure (64) shows Pumping Chamber Nr. 2 of Dry Dock Nr. 3 at Philadelphia Naval Shipyard. This graving dock was 1011'4" long and could accommodate a ship 114'2" wide with a mean low water depth of 34'4". This was a considerable graving dock that had obvious potential to accommodate even larger ships than those being designed in 1921. The dry dock had electric power as is seen in Figure (64), with its electric motor powered dewatering pumps.[168]

Things did not always go according to plan when Dry Dock Nr. 3 was used. The keel blocks had been spaced 2 foot center to center apart. Total height of the keel blocks above the dock floor was 85 ½ inches (or 7 1/8 feet high). This included the 10-inch barrier block on top of the concrete floor. In total, there were 192 keel blocks constructed out of white oak timbers with a four inch spruce softwood cap. The displacement of the *USS SOUTH CAROLINA* at the time was 16,628 tons with a trim by the stern of 3.4 feet. On May 28, 1924, the *SOUTH CAROLINA* was dry docked in Dry Dock Nr. 3. At 7:45 am the following morning, the entire keel blocking system under this battleship collapsed toward the stern. The stern fell approximately three feet.

The lessons learned from this incident helped assure that in the future adequate cribbing (or fastening the blocking together) for 25 percent of the keel blocks would be used. In addition, the use of softwood caps for the larger capital ships was minimized.[169] The spruce had plastically deformed, perhaps, due to excessive ship trim when the ship was drydocked, contributing to the failure of the blocking system the next day.

Figure (65) is a photo of the *USS ARKANSAS* in Dry Dock Nr. 3 at the Philadelphia Naval Shipyard on October 15, 1926. This photo shows one of the great advantages of graving docks. The shipyard workers can walk directly from dockside onto the ship's deck without having to go up or down steep ladders. The portal cranes on either side of the graving dock easily reached almost any spot over the ship. Both these features led to increased productivity. In Figure (65), a person can be seen sitting on the top yardarm (top center of the photo) of *ARKANSAS*, as well as sailors looking on from dockside, again without wearing hard hats (lower left of photo).

Only one more U.S. Navy owned graving dock was completed during the next 18 years after Dry Dock Nr. 3 at Philadelphia was completed in 1921. That was the graving dock at Cristobal Canal

Zone at Panama, completed in 1933. It was a relatively small dock being only 386 feet in length.

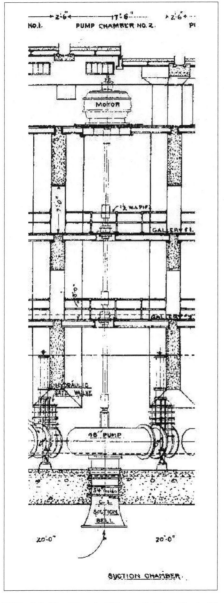

Figure 64 - Philadelphia Naval Shipyard Dry Dock Nr. 3 drawing showing electric dewatering pump. (National Archives).

Figure 65 - USS ARKANSAS in Dry Dock Nr.3 at Philadelphia Naval Shipyard October 15, 1926. (National Archives)

Chapter 15

Preparations for Another War

During this between war period, aircraft carriers emerged as the Navy's most lethal warships. Dry docks to accommodate these ships, were needed. Figure (66) shows one of the Navy's first aircraft carriers (*LEXINGTON* or *SARATOGA*) in Dry Dock Nr. 4 at the Norfolk Navy Yard. This was the only dry dock that could accommodate this size ship at that yard. The problem was that little had been done since World War I to modernize the Navy yards, other than that done as result of the National Industrial Recovery Administration, Civil Works Administration, which resulted from the Depression. The Navy yards were not ready for the upcoming war in Europe and the Pacific.

> "Although they had undergone considerable expansion during World War I, none of the yards were fully equipped to cope with the building and repair requirements of the two-ocean Navy of World War II, and most of them were congested, obsolescent, and poorly arranged."[170]

Figure 66 - Pre-World War II photo of Norfolk Naval Shipyard Dry Dock Nr. 4 with one of first aircraft carriers in the dock. (National Archives)

Larger and additional graving docks were needed for the Navy with the addition of a new class ship, the aircraft carrier (CV). In November and December of 1927, the carriers USS *SARATOGA (CV 3)* and *USS LEXINGTON (CV 2)* were commissioned. They were followed by *USS RANGER (CV 4)* in June 1934 and *USS YORKTOWN (CV 5)* in September 1937, *USS ENTERPRISE (CV 6)* in May 1938, and *USS WASP (CV 7)* in April 1940.[171] The *USS HORNET (CV 8)* was commissioned 20 October 1941.[172]

It is extremely important to note that the efforts ongoing at the private shipyards during the 30s created the ships that led to the requirements for the Navy Yard graving docks for ship repair. Newport News Shipbuilding and Dry Dock Company, (now Northrop Grumman Newport News), built the *USS RANGER (CV 4)*, *USS YORKTOWN (CV 5)*, *USS ENTERPRISE (CV 6)* and the *USS HORNET (CV 8)*. This enormous effort started with the *RANGER* in 1931. Figure (67) shows the *RANGER* being launched on February 25, 1933. This was the first aircraft carrier designed and built from the keel up, in contrast to *LEXINGTON* and *SARATOGA* which were converted from battle cruiser designs.

Figure 67 - USS RANGER (CV 4), first aircraft carrier built from the keel up, launched at Newport News Shipbuilding and Dry Dock Company February 25, 1933. (U.S. Navy Photo).[173]

This carrier construction continued for 10 years when *HORNET* was commissioned just 2 months before the Pearl Harbor attack. Three of these ships, *YORKTOWN*, *ENTERPRISE*, and *HORNET* and their air wings, changed the tide of World War II in the Pacific with the victory over the Imperial Japanese Navy at the Battle of Midway in June 1942, just 8 months after the *HORNET* was commissioned. These were just-in-time carriers built by this magnificent commercial yard!

Figure (68) is a June 1937 photo of Newport News Shipbuilding and Dry Dock Company, Newport News Virginia. The *YORKTOWN* is in the foreground preparing for sea trials. The *ENTERPRISE* is seen in the upper portion of the figure in dry dock being fitted out. This shows the dry dock capacity at this commercial yard as well. However, these dry docks were needed for part of the new construction process and could not always be counted on for ship repairs. New construction versus repair are two different priority missions the Navy must consider even today when determining dry dock availability. These are very challenging to juggle, depending on the configuration of the shipyard. Three graving docks can be seen in Figure (68) with one occupied by the *ENTERPRISE*, another by a commercial vessel, and one perhaps empty.

Figure 68 - USS YORKTOWN (CV 5) at the Newport News Shipbuilding and Dry Dock Company, Newport News, Virginia, in June 1937. USS ENTERPRISE (CV 6) is being fitted out in dry dock also seen in upper left of this figure. (U. S. Navy Photo)[174]

Aircraft carrier construction continued throughout the war at Newport News with the commissioning of the *USS ESSEX (CV 9)* December 1942. As a comparison, showing the rapidly increasing size of these carriers, *RANGER* displaced 14,500 tons, *HORNET* displaced 19,800 tons (1941), and *ESSEX* was 27,100 tons (1942). Dry dock size had to quickly accommodate the growing Navy, both in numbers and in individual ship size.

In 1936, my Grandfather, Commander Joseph Francis Daniels, USN (Ret) wrote a letter to his friend, Adm. Harold R. Stark, who became the eighth Chief of Naval Operations in 1939, suggesting the building of a Navy Yard at Terminal Island, Long Beach, California. Adm. Stark soon wrote a letter back to him stating that a shipyard at Terminal Island was not contemplated at this time.

However, the Navy's opinion soon changed. Congress started the desperately needed improvements in the Navy Yards, after twenty years of minimal funding, by passing the Naval Appropriation Act of 1938 with 20 million dollars for Navy Yard public works. World events in 1938, and the concerns over the Pacific Theater, prompted Congress and the Administration to act to correct the lack of graving docks on the West Coast.

> "In the two decades following World War I, the policies of the U.S. Navy were focused mainly on the possibility of a war in the Pacific with Japan."[175]

The Navy and the nation needed a new vision, strong will and most of all, leadership to turn the new Navy requirements into a reality. President Franklin Roosevelt found such a person in 1937. He was Commander Ben Moreel. The President was personally familiar with the talents of Commander Moreel and hand picked him to be the Chief of the Bureau of Yards and Docks, promoting him to Rear Admiral and skipping the rank of Captain.

Admiral Moreel was one of the factors that led not only to the most audacious graving dock and Navy yard building program in U.S. history, but also to the designing and building of critical forward deployed advanced based sectional floating dry docks. He also founded the Seabees. He was an incredible American who was the right man at the right time.

> "Admiral Ben Moreell, the first Chief of the Bureau of Yards and Docks [who was] not a graduate of the Naval Academy, was the founding father of the Navy's famous Seabees and largely responsible for overseeing the Bureau's vast construction programs, both domestic and overseas, during World War II."[176]

The Navy also made a comprehensive review of the needs of the Navy yards. The Navy determined that needed improvements would require a budget of 145 million dollars to modernize and upgrade these yards.

> "In the fall of 1938, the Chief of the Bureau of Yards and Docks prepared a comprehensive plan for the improvement of the naval shore establishment ... This plan .... issued on January 1, 1939, ... proposed $75,000,000 ... for correction of accumulated deficiencies at the Navy Yards, and $70,000,000 ... for yard improvements."[177]

These navy yard improvements were, once again, tied to new ship construction. The Navy was growing as a result of the Vinson Fleet Expansion Bill of 1938. Graving dock construction started again primarily in Hawaii and the West Coast. Also, funding for the last two United States Navy yards (Hunters Point and Terminal Island) was provided under the "Public Works, Navy" Appropriation in 1939 and 1940.

The first project initiated after these appropriations of funds in 1938 was another graving dock at the Puget Sound Navy Yard. Their 867-foot dock was the only dry dock on the West Coast at the time that could handle a battleship. The second dock was to be over 1,000 feet in length to accommodate the longer ships being designed. Work started on what was to become Dry Dock Nr. 4 at Puget Sound Navy Yard in fall 1938. A year later, construction was started on another large graving dock at Puget Sound.

At the New York Navy Yard, a modification to Dry Dock Nr. 4 commenced. The dock had to be notched, lengthening it by 32 feet to allow the construction of the *USS NORTH CAROLINA*. Because the original dry dock construction was unique (concrete wall caissons were used around the perimeter, the floor was supported by pneumatic caissons, and the notched area had treacherous site conditions), the entire extension of the dock was sunk as a unit using compressed air methods.[178]

In December 1939, a "lump-sum" contract was awarded for two more graving docks at Pearl Harbor, adjacent to Dry Dock Nr. 1, that had been in operation since 1919. As opposed to Dry Dock Nr. 4 at the Norfolk Navy Yard, finished after World War II, these docks would be completed in time to be invaluable during World War II. However, they were not completed prior to the attack by the Japanese on December 7, 1941. Dry Dock Nr. 2 was designed to handle the battleships and aircraft carriers similar to Dry Dock Nr. 1.[179]

Dry Dock Nr. 3 opened at Mare Island Naval Shipyard in 1940. This 693 foot long dry dock was primarily for destroyers and submarines. In April 1940, construction started on Dry Dock Nr. 4 at Mare Island. It was 435 feet long and also designed for destroyers and submarines.[180]

The two graving docks at Puget Sound opened in time for World War II in 1941. These were Dry Docks Nr. 4 and 5 and were 997 feet and 1030 feet long respectively. Dry Dock Nr. 4 is shown in Figure (69) when it opened in October 1940. These graving docks were built in the dry area behind a cofferdam.

Figure 69 - Puget Sound Navy Yard Dry Dock Nr. 4 opening in 1940. (U. S. Navy Photo).

"William Henry Mueser, who became a world renowned civil engineer, was a partner assigned to represent the firm, Moran, Maurice & Proctor, in the Dry Dock Engineers, a combination of four firms assembled to carry out the design of major graving docks for the U. S. Navy's Bureau of Yards and Docks. He was involved in the design and construction of many dry docks, including the one at Bremerton, Washington, which was the world's deepest and largest in volume of ship space."[181]

Planning for the *IOWA* class battleships (55,000 tons) and what was going to be the *MONTANA* class battleships (70,000 tons) had begun. Their size necessitated the designing and construction of huge building dry docks. Construction of what was called "superdocks" was started in Norfolk and Philadelphia in June 1940.[182] These massive graving docks would be 1092 feet long and 150 feet wide. The new graving dock in Norfolk was contracted under the same contract as Dry Docks Nr. 4 & 5 at Philadelphia.

On June 17, 1940, exactly 107 years after the docking of the first ship in the United States, the Chief of Naval Operations, Admiral Harold R. Stark, testified before Congress requesting 4 billion dollars to build a two-ocean navy. This was the Naval Expansion Act signed into law by President Roosevelt on July 19, 1940.[183] From July 1940 to December 1941, the Navy's Bureau of Ships transferred more than 250 million dollars from the "two-ocean Navy" funding to the Bureau of Yards and Docks to expedite the upgrade and expansion of the Navy yards. The Navy in real fiscal terms realized that there was an inexorable link between the fleet and her Navy yards. Congress appropriated an additional 33 million dollars directly for the Navy Yards. Ten million of this money was to expand the New York Navy Yard to include the Bayonne facility across the Hudson in New Jersey.

Part of the 1940 appropriation for "Public Works, Navy" was 6 million dollars for the acquisition and initial development of what was to become Hunters Point and Terminal Island Navy Yards. These were that last two Navy yards (later called Naval Shipyards) ever to be constructed for the United States Navy.

In August 1940, work was started on the Terminal Island facility, what was later called the Long Beach Naval Shipyard. In

November 1940, work commenced at Hunters Point in San Francisco.

In January 1941, a Navy Board, interestingly enough called the "Hepburn Board" (no relation), headed by Rear Admiral John W. Greenslade, recommended that the Navy's shore establishment on each coast of the United States be able to maintain the entire Navy. The size of the Navy contemplated was over 2000 ships![184]

After this, graving dock construction went into an historical frenzy. In April 1941, Dry Dock Nr. 1 (435 feet long and 91 feet wide) was placed under contract at the Portsmouth Navy Yard. Also in April, a small building dock, Dry Dock Nr. 2, was placed under contract at the Charleston Navy Yard in South Carolina. At the Boston Navy Yard, in October 1941, work started on a shipbuilding drydock (518 feet long and 91 feet wide) for escort vessels.

In mid 1941, more shipbuilding docks were started at the Philadelphia and New York Navy Yards. The "tremie" method was used for pouring and casting concrete underwater. This led to these docks being completed and ready for laying keels in 17 to 21 months. This compared to previous methods that required 3 to 8 years of construction time.[185] This was one of the most important technological developments in graving dock construction. It allowed an enormous rate increase in the graving dock completions just before and during World War II.

The tremie method included dredging over two million cubic yards of material and placing half a million cubic yards of concrete in the graving dock floor and walls underwater at the New York Navy Yard. This work started in 1941 and completed in 1942 and was described by the Navy's Bureau of Yards and Docks:

> "Six dredges were used to remove 2,300,000 cubic yards of material, at a maximum rate of 25,000 cubic yards per day, to a general depth of 63 depth feet, and a maximum depth of 72 feet, below mean low water. For the dry docks, a 2-foot layer of crushed rock was deposited and carefully leveled with a heavy drag. Pile supports were required under the entire dock structures. More than 12,000 steel H-piles weighing 74 pounds per foot, from 30 to 70 feet long, were driven under

water to 37.5-ton minimum bearing from floating drivers. Tremie forms were used for the floors and lower sidewalls. The floor forms were 14 feet wide, 20 feet high, and 190 feet long, open top and bottom, and were prefabricated steel box trusses with corrugated steel sheathing and with the required reinforcement built in. The wall forms were similar, but smaller, and included built-in frames to which steel piling could be attached to complete the sidewall cofferdam. ... Concrete was mixed at a central mixing plant, served by belt-conveyor bridge from aggregate bins .... Cement was delivered in bulk and blown to the storage bins. Peak daily requirements were fourteen 800-ton barges of aggregates and two 5,000-barrel barges of bulk cement. Concrete was delivered by pumping through a system of 8-inch pipes, with booster pumps needed, for a maximum distance of 1100 feet to the tremie barges, where it was discharged through hoppers into eight tremie pipes which could he raised and lowered as required. The concrete in a form, aggregating 1660 cubic yards, was placed in a continuous pour at a controlled rate in nine hours. More than 500,000 cubic yards of tremie concrete was placed. The outer ends of the docks were built within sheet pile cofferdams. Temporary cofferdams were built across the dock, about 700 feet from the head wall, to permit starting ship construction before the outer ends were completed."[186]

Also in October 1941, Congress appropriated the funds for dry dock construction at Bayonne, New Jersey. This dock was to be 1092 feet long and 150 feet wide and the tremie method of concrete construction was used to construct this enormous graving dock as well. A contract for the construction of a fourth graving dock at Pearl Harbor was signed on October 4, 1941, just two months before the attack.

Fortunately, as of December 7, 1941, many of the projects in the Navy Yards were available for use for they were soon to be desperately needed. Their early availability directly enabled ship construction and repair to ramp up much quicker than would have occurred if these facilities were still just land fill, as much of them were before the projects started.

In the Philippines, concern about the security of the floating dry dock, *DEWEY*, at Subic Bay (Olongapo) grew rapidly in the summer of 1941. Fort Wint was assigned with the protection of the dry dock.

> "Situated at the mouth of Subic Bay, on beautiful Grande Island, Fort Wint was ideally located to defend one of the world's great natural harbors against enemy warships. The Fort's importance was four fold. It (1) protected the Navy's small base and the Dry Dock Dewey at Olongapo, (2) protected Bataan's back door from enemy naval and amphibious attacks, (3) prevented enemy forces from using the harbor for a supply base only a few miles from our forces on Bataan, and (4) provided early warning of enemy ships and aircraft proceeding south towards Bataan and Manila Bay."[187]

Major General George F. Moore, USA assumed command of the Harbor Defenses of Manila and Subic Bays on February 14, 1941. In addition to the Army's harbor defense efforts, General Moore reported that the U.S. Navy had completed a number of defensive preparations during the summer and fall of 1941. This, including the movement of the floating dry dock *DEWEY* to a more secure mooring site.

> "The ... dry dock *"Dewey"* was towed from Olongapo to a better *protected* location in Mariveles Bay opposite Corregidor and an anti-submarine net installed across the entrance to Mariveles Harbor."[188]

Chapter 16

World War II Begins

The *USS SHAW* was in a floating dry dock at Pearl Harbor on December 7, 1941. This was an unfortunate place to be that Sunday morning. After being bombed, the forward magazine of *SHAW* ignited and caused one of the most famous explosions of the attack to be photographed shown in Figure (70). It later became the policy of the Navy not to allow ships in dry dock with their magazine full of ammunition. The Navy could not afford the loss of the dry dock as a national asset, let alone the ship itself.

> "*SHAW* was in Floating *Dry dock Number Two* when hit by three bombs from the same dive-bombers that attacked *NEVADA* about 0850. ... The third bomb was of the same type and passed through the bridge. It exploded in the wardroom pantry, and ruptured the fuel oil tanks... The heat from this oil fire caused the forward magazine to blow up. This wrecked the forward part of the ship as far back as frame 65. When the floating dry dock sank, the forward section of the ship went down with it, but the area from frame 60 aft was buoyant and remained afloat."[189]

Figure 70 - Forward magazine of USS SHAW exploding while in the floating dry dock at Pearl Harbor Navy Yard December 7, 1941. (U.S. Navy Photo)

The floating dry dock was evidently ordered flooded. It had experienced damage and did not ballast down evenly and listed heavily to one side.[190]

> "*SHAW* was originally reported as a total loss but its machinery was in good condition. ... the forward part was entirely cut off and the portion abaft frame 60 was docked on the Yard's marine railway on 19 December. ... [A false bow] was installed on *SHAW* on 26 January 1942 when the ship was subsequently docked [back] on *Floating Dry dock Number Two*."[191]

One account says Floating Dry Dock Nr. 2 was not sunk by the damage but was intentionally sunk for protection:

> "*Floating Dry Dock Number Two* was subjected to a heavy blitz about 0850. The Japanese planes were dive-bombers dropping 250 kilogram bombs, five of which fell near the floating dry dock. She was submerged for protection."[192]

The bombs and explosions on *SHAW* put 155 holes in the floating dry dock. Divers welded up the holes and were able to raise the dry dock on January 9, 1942 just a month after the attack. For a month, she had rested on the bottom with a 15-degree list. By January 25th, she was ready to work and the next day actually docked what was left of the *SHAW* as her first customer ship. The *SHAW's* engineering spaces were in good enough shape to refurbish, and while in dry dock, a new temporary bow was installed so *SHAW* could return stateside for a complete reconstruction.

The Japanese recognized the mistake of not destroying the dry docks at Pearl Harbor Naval Shipyard during their attack December 7, 1941, although, they attempted to do so. Two hundred yards east of where the destroyer *USS SHAW (DD373)* was attached in the floating dry dock, the *USS CASSIN (DD372)*, the *USS DOWNES (DD375)*, and the *USS PENNSYLVANIA (BB38)* were attacked while in Dry Dock Nr. 1.[193] Figure (71) shows the two destroyers, burned and wrecked on the inboard end of the graving dock forward of the *PENNSYLVANIA*.

The *CASSIN*, which was later rebuilt, is shown in Figure (72) capsized in the drydock. Flooding of the graving dock led to the capsizing of the ship. However, with the fires and explosions it was an obvious risk management decision. The problem with the *CASSIN* capsizing was that it took longer to make Dry Dock Nr. 1 operational again. Fortunately, Dry Dock Nr. 1 itself suffered minimal damage.

Figure 71 - December 7, 1941 at the Pearl Harbor Navy Yard, two destroyers, the USS CASSIN (DD372) and the USS DOWNES (DD375) were in Dry Dock Nr. 1 with the battleship USS PENNSYLVANIA (BB38)

Figure 72 - USS CASSIN under salvage in the same drydock attacked at Pearl Harbor Navy Yard January 23, 1942. (Naval Historical Center)

CINCPAC also recognized the relative good fortune in the Japanese sparing the Navy Yard of crippling damage. Having the dry docks available at the site of the attack allowed Admiral Nimitz to reconstitute his fleet. Figure (73) is a plan of Pearl Harbor Naval Shipyard. The locations of Dry Docks Nr. 1, Nr. 2, Nr. 3, and Nr. 4 are shown. Dry Dock Nr. 3 and Nr. 4 were completed later in the war. The December 7, 1941 mooring site of the Floating Dry Dock Nr.2 was near Dry Dock Nr. 3.

Meanwhile in the Philippines, the Marines and the Navy had their hands full protecting the floating dry dock *DEWEY*, still considered an essential asset.

> "After the movement of the 4th Marines to Corregidor in December, there were still Marines on Bataan. Two antiaircraft batteries operated in the Mariveles area and formed part of a naval defense battalion for the southern coast of Bataan. Battery A, commanded by First Lieutenant William F. Hogaboom, was stationed at the Mariveles Quarantine Station, protecting an old Dewey Dry Dock. The battery consisted of two officers and 80 men and was armed with nine machine guns for low level antiaircraft defense. One Navy

officer and 65 sailors were attached to the battery. Battery C, under First Lieutenant Wilfred D. Holdredge was posted in an abandoned rice paddy between the Navy Section Base and the village of Mariveles. The battery was composed of four 3-inch antiaircraft guns and had an ensign and 40 sailors attached."[196]

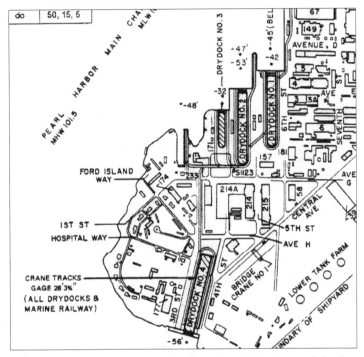

Figure 73 - Pearl Harbor Naval Shipyard with locations of the four graving dry docks.[195]

Fortunately for the Navy, Dry Dock Nr. 2 was almost complete on December 7th. Although unfinished, she had a caisson in place and was able to drydock the cruiser *USS HELENA* on December 10, 1941. *HELENA* undocked on December 21st. The graving dock was completed while being used. This was a case where a graving dock was completed "just in time!"[194] To complete the docking of the *HELENA*, Dry Dock Nr. 2's drainage pumps and other auxiliary pumps had to be used for dewatering, as the dry dock's primary dewatering pumps were still not operational.

The U.S. Naval and Marine forces tried to defend the *DEWEY* the night before Bataan fell. The dock had been towed to the bottom of the Mariveles harbor to better protect it.

The station ship *USS NEW YORK* was scuttled while the *DEWEY* was still being defended. Finally, the night before Bataan fell on April 8, 1942 the *DEWEY YFD-1* was blown up to prevent it from getting into Japanese hands.[197, 198, 199] The Japanese evidently successfully raised the dock that was subsequently resunk again by American aircraft.[200] She had survived a tow half way around the world, and did not succumb easily to the destruction of the battlefield.

The lack of forward deployed dry docks in safe harbors at the beginning of World War II in the Western Pacific led to the damage and eventual loss of a Navy warship to the enemy. That ship was the *USS STEWART (DE 238)*. On February 21, 1942, after sustaining damage to her steering system during the Battle of Java Sea, she was ordered to proceed to Surabaya for drydocking. During the docking in a commercial yard there, the sideblocking system or shoring failed disastrously causing the ship to capsize in the dry dock causing severe damage.[201]

The *STEWART* suffered hull, shafting and propeller damage, in addition interior flooding occurred. She was unable to escape aerial attacks by the Japanese and was damaged further. The U.S. Navy ordered her destruction either February 23rd or March 2, 1942. The destruction was not confirmed and the ship eventually was recovered and refitted by the Japanese Navy. No report is given, although, the Japanese might have used the dry dock that was there for this refitting.

Chapter 17

On the Road to Recovery and Ultimate Victory

The failure of the Japanese to completely destroy Pearl's drydocking capability left the U.S. Navy with a first class repair facility in the mid-Pacific. Having the dry docks available at Pearl Harbor was one of the single most important factors in the recovery of the U.S. Navy Fleet after the devastating attack. Just like the Confederates at the beginning of the Civil War when they salvaged the *MERRIMACK* in Dry Dock Nr. 1, lack of dry dock destruction directly led to future naval victories.

The dry docks at Pearl Harbor soon played a key role in the next major naval battles of World War II in the Pacific. After the Battle of Coral Sea, the carrier *USS YORKTOWN (CV-5)* was in desperate need of repair. Figure (74) shows *YORKTOWN* in Dry Dock Nr. 1 at the Pearl Harbor Navy Yard one week before she was sunk during the Battle of Midway. *YORKTOWN's* presence at the Battle of Midway June 1942 however, was a key factor in the decisive victory for the United States over Japan.

Figure 74 - USS YORKTOWN (CV-5) In dry dock at Pearl Harbor, repairing her damage from the Battle of Coral Sea, just prior to sailing for Midway. She was sunk less than a week later during the Battle of Midway June 1942.[202] (Naval Historical Center)

Dry Dock Nr. 3 at Pearl Harbor was smaller and designed to accommodate destroyers and submarines It was only half finished on December 7, 1941. This dock was only 497 feet long and not complete until 1942.

Between the time Dry Dock Nr. 3 was completed at Pearl in 1942, and the opening of Dry Dock Nr 4, a marine railway was also constructed at the Pearl Harbor Navy Yard with a capacity of 3000 tons with a length of 836 feet. It would accommodate destroyers and submarines.[203]

Dry Dock Nr. 4 was not fully ready for service for another year and a half and her first docking did not occur until October 6, 1943. This dock was 1088 feet long and her construction was one of the many magnificent achievements in graving dock construction in World War II. However, it did take half the war before it was in service.

From 1938 to 1945, the Navy expended more than 590 million dollars in construction and improvements in the Navy yards. This period was the largest expansion of drydocking capability in United States history. It was necessary, for by mid-1945 there were thousands of ships in active commission. Much of the construction was done at private shipyards during World War II. However, the volume of work imposed on the Navy yards during the War was of proportions undreamt of before the war.

The biblical building rate of docking facilities continued in earnest into 1942. In January 1942, construction commenced at the Philadelphia Navy Yard for 3000-ton marine railway and on a second one in February. There was also a change to the contract for the second 1092-foot graving dock. The depth over the sill was changed to 43 feet 6 inches from 40 inches. The two 1092 feet long graving docks, Dry Docks Nr 4 and 5, at Philadelphia required the removal of over 2.8 million cubic yards of material.

The tremie method was used to pour the concrete for the two graving docks in Philadelphia. These graving docks were needed so urgently that Dry Dock Nr. 4 had a temporary cofferdam constructed so building battleships could commence even before the graving dock was completed. Dry Dock Nr. 4 completed in 1941 and Dry Dock Nr. 5 completed in 1942.

A similar dry dock at Norfolk was also completed in 1942, and a cofferdam had also been placed in this dock to allow ship construction to proceed. Figure (75) is a side by side map of Philadelphia Navy Yard and the Norfolk Navy Yard. Dry Docks Nr 4 and 5 at Philadelphia and Dry Dock Nr. 8 at Norfolk were the graving docks built under the same contract to the same dimensions, 1092 feet long.

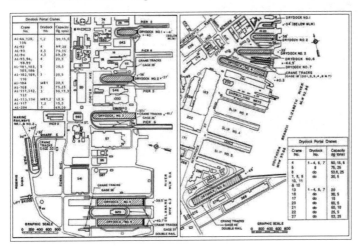

Figure 75 - Map of Philadelphia Navy Yard (left) and Norfolk Navy Yard (right). (U.S. Navy).[204]

Dry Dock Nr. 1 at the Long Beach Navy Yard was also 1092 feet long. It also completed in 1942. This dock was later named the Moreell Dock, after Admiral Ben Moreell, Chief of the Bureau of Yards and Docks during World War II. I drydocked the *USS MISSOURI (BB 63)* in this same dry dock, in 1984, 42 years later. Figure (76) is a photo of Dry Dock Nr. 1 at Long Beach with an insert showing the *USS MISSOURI (BB 63)* dry docked in 1984. For this drydocking, the *MISSOURI* required 450 blocks on the dock floor.

Because of the *MISSOURI's* flat bottom, all the build up was a single standard concrete block height of 5 feet. The ship had been laid up as a museum for 30 years after serving in the Korean War. There were over 169 projections sticking below the baseline of the ship such as cofferdams over the sea chests. All these projections had to be identified and avoided when this great ship landed on the blocks in August 1984.

Figure 76 - Long Beach (Terminal Island) Navy Yard Dry Dock Nr. 1 opened 1942. Insert is USS MISSOURI (BB63) in this graving dock in August 1984. (U.S. Navy Photo).

At Hunters Point Navy Yard, another of the 1092 feet long graving docks, Dry Dock Nr. 4, was completed in 1942. Figure (77) shows this dock getting ready to test.

Figure 77 - Hunters Point Navy Yard. (U.S. Navy Photo)

During the War years of 1942 to 1944, the United States Navy put 26 graving docks into service, 13 of these in 1942 and another 13 in 1943. Basically, the U.S. completed a graving dock a month for two years running. This accomplishment was truly a remarkable and unbelievable achievement. At no time in the history of the United States had so many graving docks been put into service. Not even close. In fact, up to that point there had been only 29 graving docks put into service in the previous 108 years! This is a tremendous testimony to the civil engineers and labor force that made this possible in a time of national emergency.

Figure (78) shows the New York Navy Yard in full swing in 1944 with all graving docks completed. It was a battleship building yard and a critical repair yard, contributing such ships as the *USS MISSOURI (BB 63)* to the war effort. *MISSOURI* was the location of the Japanese surrender to allied forces when the ship was anchored in Tokyo Bay on September 2, 1945.

Photo # NH 93234 New York Navy Yard, Brooklyn, NY, 9 March 1944

Figure 78 - New York Navy yard with all graving docks completed on March 9, 1944. (U.S. Navy Photo)

Table (2) is a listing of these 26 graving docks put into service during World War II. This was extraordinary achievement by Admiral Ben Moreell, CEC, and his tens of thousands of engineers and trades people that made this possible. It was an epic moment in history by Bureau of Yards and Docks, the United States Navy, the engineering firms and contractors, and the American people.

Table 2 - Graving docks completed during World War II (1942 through 1944)

Location	Dry Dock Number	Date Completed	Length (ft)
BAYONNE NJ	7	1942	1092
BOSTON	5	1942	516
LONG BEACH	1	1942	1092
MARE ISLAND	4	1942	435
NEW YORK	5	1942	1092
NEW YORK	6	1942	1092
NORFOLK	8	1942	1092
PEARL HARBOR	3	1942	496
PHILADELPHIA	5	1942	1092
PORTSMOUTH	3	1942	492
SAN DIEGO	1	1942	693
SAN FRANCISCO	4	1942	1092
SAN JUAN PR	1	1942	654
CHARLESTON	3	1943	365
CHARLESTON	4	1943	365
LONG BEACH	2	1943	687
LONG BEACH	3	1943	687
PEARL HARBOR	4	1943	1088
PORTSMOUTH	2	1943	740
SOUTH BOSTON	4	1943	693
BALBOA CZ	3	1944	219
BALBOA CZ	2	1944	424
ROOSEVELT ROADS PR	1	1944	1088
SAN FRANCISCO	5	1944	420
SAN FRANCISCO	6	1944	420
SAN FRANCISCO	7	1944	420

"It was due to [Admiral Moreell's] unrelenting energy that "the fleet received support in degree and kind unprecedented in the history of naval warfare", as stated in the citation of his Distinguished Service Medal, presented to [Admiral] Moreell in 1945."[205]

Chapter 18

Floating Dry Docks During World War II and Beyond

Floating dry docks also saw considerable use during World War II. There were 147 floating dry docks of various capacities constructed and put into service during the war. Only three were in use prior to the War. These dry docks provided many advantages to the United States Navy during the war years. The first was mobility. They could be moved to where they were needed. Having adequate numbers of graving docks, floating dry docks, and marine railways stateside and in Hawaii was not enough. The fleet needed dry docks close to where the action was.

The U.S. Navy forward deployed many floating dry docks during World War II. Mr. Volney E. Cook, Assistant Manager of Ships and Fleet Facilities Branch Head of the Drydocking and Mooring Facilities Section of the Bureau of Yards and Docks, Navy Department, wrote in 1957 of the expansion of the number of floating dry docks during World War II:

> "During the tremendous expansion program just prior to and during World War II, many dry docks of all types were built. This expansion occurred with greatest force in the floating-dry dock portion of the program where the number of floating dry docks increased from 3 to more than 150. The sizes and types ranged from small one-piece concrete structures having a lifting capacity of 400 tons to the very large AFDB docks built in sections with a lifting capacity of 90,000 tons nominal (100,000 tons maximum)."[206]

Floating dry docks provided critical ship repair facilities close to the theater of operation. Many of these dry docks such as ARDs (Auxiliary Repair Dry Dock) were built to withstand dangerous conditions. An ARD was designed to be towed. It had a bow and a flying bridge and a closed end of the dry dock which was shut after a ship entered. It had berthing and messing for the crew and was basically self sufficient once put into position and occasionally replenished. ARD 1 was towed to Pearl Harbor where it served throughout World War II. Many of these

ARD floating dry docks actually saw combat action against the Japanese.

There are 5 classes of U.S. Navy floating dry docks. Table (3) lists these floating dry docks as they existed February 1, 1955.

Table 3 - Classes and numbers of U.S. Navy Floating dry docks as of February 1, 1955 (U.S. Navy).[207]

CLASS OF FLOATING DRY DOCK	NUMBER 1 February 1955	LIFTING CAPACITY RANGE (TONS)	CONSTRUCTION FINISH DATE RANGE
AFDB	7	55,000-90,000	1943-1945
AFDM	10	15,000-18,000	1942-1945
AFDL	41	1,000-6500	1943-1955
ARD	28	3500	1942-1944
YFD	20	2,000-20,000	1934-1943

Captain Harry A. Jackson, USN (ret), a prominent retired naval engineering duty officer and submarine designer, discussed Mr. Voney Cook's paper "General Discussion of Floating Dry docks" and mentioned the following about the critical contribution of floating dry docks during World War II:

> "During World War II, over 7000 ships were docked in forward areas. Each docking contributed to the successful conclusion of the naval war."[208]

Figure (79) shows an AFDB floating dry dock that was forward deployed to Espiritu Santo, New Hebrides during World War II. Captain Jackson served as the Docking Officer and Repair Officer on this dry dock. These docks were originally designated ABSD (Advanced Base Section Dry Dock).[209] Note that this ABSD had ten sections, each of which was towed separately from the United States and then assembled at the forward deployed location.

The *USS PENNSYLVANIA (BB 38)*, one of the survivors of Pearl Harbor, was placed in an ABSD in the Pacific later in World War II for maintenance and bottom painting.[210] Captain W. Mack Angas, CEC, USN, made the following remark in the November 1945 edition of *Popular Science* in an article entitled "Seagoing Navy Yard Follows the Fleet" regarding the role of ABSDs in the Western Pacific during World War II:

"Having such a dock right with the fleet when you want it fulfills an admiral's dream. Superdreadnoughts, in advance combat areas, thus are spared voyages of thousands of miles to permanent repair bases at Hawaii and on the U.S. Coasts. The difference in time that the ship is out of service may determine whether or not it can take part in a decisive battle, and its timely arrival could add the needed power for victory. In fact, mobile "hospitals" for battleships seem likely to have a profound effect upon naval tactics of the future – a study that no nation dares neglect, no matter how remote the prospect of war."[211]

I talked to Captain Harry Jackson, USN (Ret) on January 26, 2000 about his experiences as a docking officer. He told me that he was the docking officer of the Espiritu Santo dry dock, ABSD 1, and later ABSD-3 at Guam. During World War II, Captain Jackson drydocked 300 ships. One was the *USS NEW MEXICO (BB 40)* which had been damaged in the propeller area by a kamikaze. One liberty ship he drydocked had run over a mine and it had an 8 inch hog midships. He did a complete forward area repair on this ship, including virtually cutting the ship in two and welding it back together.

Rear Admiral W. H Smith (CEC) USN (Ret), made the following tribute to Captain J. T. Reside, CEC, USNR who directed the Drydocking and Mooring Facilities Section of the Bureau of Yards and Docks during World War II. "His ... contributions to the fleet in the field of drydocking during the strenuous years of the War were enormous."[212]

The *USS SOUTH DAKOTA* was one of the many ships Captain Jackson drydocked in the ABSD-3 at Guam. According to one of the officers on the *USS SOUTH DAKOTA* at the time, Colonel Merrill J. King, Jr., US Army Medical Corp (Ret), the ship had run aground on a coral reef damaging the propellers.

The forward deployed dry docks were critical to the success of the invasion of Okinawa. The fleet was being subjected in incessant attacks for weeks by the kamikazes. The fleet suffered tremendous damage and the forward floating dry docks were there to repair the ships. This allowed in theater repairs to be accomplished in a minimum time, allowing the ships to get back into action. They acted as a force multiplier allowing recently damaged ships to reengage.

On these ABSDs, United States Navy sailors did all dry dock operations and ship repairs. These dry docks were self-contained with repair shops, berthing and messing. The drydocking officer, such as Captain Jackson, did all the drydocking calculations and was completely responsible for the execution of all drydocking evolutions. This was typical of duties of an engineering duty officer assigned as drydocking officers on these huge floating dry docks in forward areas. The ABSD-3 that was in Guam, was the floating dry dock Bath Iron Works used until December 2000 at Portland, Maine to install the sonar domes on the *ARLEIGH BURKE* class DDG's during new construction. I looked at ABSD-3 on January 29, 2000 at Portland, Maine. It had only 9 of the original 10 sections left. The designation ABSD-3 was still proudly displayed yet coated in a blue paint instead of the original haze gray.

This floating drydock ended its long association with the United States Navy in April 2001. It was cut in half and five sections were heavy lifted to Croatia by the heavy lift ship *BLUE MARLIN* when she was sold to that country by the State of Maine. Bath Iron Works then brought their new land level transfer facility and their new floating dry dock that was built in China on line in September 2001.

Figure 79 - USS ANTELOPE (IX-109) In the floating dry dock ABSD-1 at Espiritu Santo, New Hebrides, January 8, 1945. Also in the dry dock, astern of Antelope is USS LST-120. YF-326 is the nearest of the yardcraft on the right, moored to ABSD-1. (U.S. Navy Photos)

Figure (79) and Figure (80) are photographs of the docking process for the *ANTELOPE* in ABSD 1January 5, 1945. Line handling was manually done with capstans to provide inhaul and centering power.

Figure 80 - USS ANTELOPE (IX-109) Entering the floating dry dock ABSD-1 at Espiritu Santo, New Hebrides, January 5, 1945. (U.S. Navy Photo)

Figure (81) is a photo of a U.S. Navy owned floating dry dock *USS RESOLUTE* (AFDM 10) that was still being used at the Naval Operating Base Norfolk, Virginia in 2002. The *RESOLUTE* is electric powered. Diesel generators supply the power when disconnected from the pier. In *RESOLUTE's* case at the Norfolk Operating Base, there was enough water depth at the mooring site to accommodate the submerged dry dock without having to move the dock. Side blocks are hauled in via chains from the wing walls.

Figure 81 - USS RESOLUTE (AFDM 10) at the Naval Operating Base (NOB) Norfolk, Virginia 1996 (U.S. Navy Photo)

The *RESOLUTE* as shown in Figure (81) is near the minimum stability condition as her dock floor is just covered with water. At this point, the dry dock has the minimum waterplane area and thus the minimum righting moment. This occurs when the dry dock is being ballasted down in preparation for docking a ship or when it is deballasting and the dock floor starts to come out of the water. When this occurs, there is a drastic reduction in the righting moment of the dry dock and the entire dry dock can quickly take on a heel if the liquid load of the dry dock is not carefully monitored.

After World War II, the U.S. Navy placed an AFDB (Large Auxiliary Floating Dry Dock) at Subic Bay, Philippines at the Ship Repair Facility. She was capable of drydocking battleships. Another AFDB was placed at Holy Loch Scotland in 1961 for the drydocking of fleet ballistic missile submarines. This floating dry dock was the *USS LOS ALAMOS (AFDB 7)*. It had five pontoons on which sat the wing walls. Figure (82) is a cross section of an AFDB. The pontoons not only contained the ballast tanks, but the machinery and pumps to operate the dry dock. The berthing and messing areas were also in these pontoons.

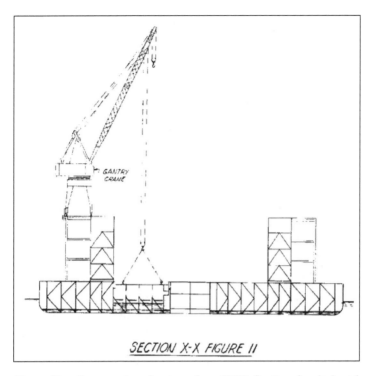

Figure 82 - Cross section drawing of an AFDB floating dry dock with wing wall crane. (U.S. Navy drawing).

The USS LOS ALAMOS stayed at Holy Loch, Scotland until the early 1990s. It was lifted onto a heavy lift ship in the early 1990s and brought back to the James River Inactive Ships facility in Virginia. In 1996, five sections were towed to Brownsville Texas for use by a private shipyard.

In during the Vietnam War, dry docks were essential. The AFDB at Subic Bay, Philippines was in almost constant use throughout the war. There was an AFDL (Small Auxiliary Floating Dry Dock) placed at DaNang, South Vietnam for small craft and yard vessel repair until that facility was lost to enemy forces.

> "A small craft repair facility and a floating dry dock (AFDL) helped keep NSA [Naval Support Activity] vessels in working order... The logistic establishment at DaNang functioned with growing efficiency by mid-1968 as it built new port and shore facilities."[213]

Private yards found floating dry docks attractive as they were easily purchased and sold as the economic climate dictated. The shipyards did not have to give up prime water front property or commit to a permanent structure, as is the case with a marine railway or graving dock. Dredging was usually required depending on the depth of water in the vicinity of the shipyard. In some cases for a drydocking evolution, the shipyard must move the floating dry dock using tugs or mooring system to a location with adequate depth in the harbor not adjacent to the yard.

Auxiliary diesels power the dock's electrical generators for the deballasting pumps, electrical service loads, fire pumps, and valve controls. On Navy manned floating dry docks, the docks are self-contained with berthing and messing for the crew along with workshops, offices, and dry dock control stations.

The *SPRUANCE* Class destroyer joined the United States Navy in the 1970s. This entire ship class was built by one shipyard, Ingalls Shipbuilding at Pascagoula, Mississippi. This required the shipyard to build a fabrication, assembly, and launching facility to accommodate such a large ship construction program. The shipyard used a floating dry dock to launch the ship. Figure (83) shows the *SPRUANCE* in place on the floater prior to sea trials.

In this position, the floating dry dock is sitting on piers next to the quay wall. The wing wall is removed so the ship can translate sideways on a cradle and rail system from the shipyard land assembly area to the dry dock. Once the wingwall is replaced, the dry dock is deballisted and moved with the ship on it to the area dredged for submergence of the dry dock. In 2001, Bath Iron Works of Bath, Maine, opened a similar facility as was mentioned for the construction of the DDG 51, and DDX classes of ships. Ingalls is still using their facility building DDG 51 and LHD class ships and will probably use it for DDX construction.

Figure 83 - USS SPRUANCE (DD-963) in the floating dry dock at the Ingalls shipyard, Pascagoula, Mississippi, while being prepared for builders' trials, circa January 1975. (U.S. Navy Photo)

Chapter 19

Post World War II High Water Mark for U.S. Navy Graving Docks

By 1955, the Korean War was over and the Navy stabilized under the threat of the Cold War. In 1955, there were 11 U.S. Naval Shipyards that provided repair sites for a fleet consisting of 142 submarines, 16 attack carriers, 3 battleships, 10 heavy cruisers, 3 light cruisers, 249 destroyers, 64 escort ships, and 175 amphibious ships.[214] The U.S. Naval Shipyards were Pearl Harbor, Puget Sound, Hunters Point, Mare Island, Long Beach, Charleston, Norfolk, Philadelphia, Brooklyn, Boston, and Portsmouth.

In addition, the U.S. Navy owned a graving dock at the Naval Base at San Diego, four in the Canal Zone, and one in Puerto Rico. This book does not go into the other foreign dry docks available to the U.S. Navy post World War II such as the substantial Japanese graving docks at Yokosuka, Japan.

Table (4) lists all of what were U.S. Navy owned graving docks that existed February 1, 1955. These 55 dry docks had all been put into service by 1944. Some of the graving docks were located outside U.S. Naval Shipyards but were at U.S. Navy bases, and some of these were located outside the continental United States and Hawaii such as Puerto Rico and Panama.[215] The dry docks are listed in order of their completion dates. In addition to these 55 graving docks in 1955 there were 12 marine railways and 106 floating dry docks available for U.S. Navy use, including Subic Bay, Philippines and Guam.

Table 4 - All U.S. Navy owned graving docks, locations, dry dock number, date completed, and the length of the dock that existed February 1, 1955.[216]

Location	Dry Dock Number	Date Completed	Length
NORFOLK	1	1833	325
BOSTON	1	1833	403
NEW YORK	1	1851	349
NORFOLK	2	1889	495

Location	Dry Dock Number	Date Completed	Length
NEW YORK	2	1890	465
SAN FRANCISCO	2	1904	742
BOSTON	2	1905	717
PORTSMOUTH	1	1905	435
CHARLESTON	1	1907	597
NORFOLK	3	1908	723
PHILADELPHIA	2	1908	744
MARE ISLAND	2	1910	741
NEW YORK	4	1913	702
PUGET SOUND	2	1913	867
BALBOA CZ	1	1916	1076
SAN FRANCISCO	3	1916	1005
NORFOLK	6	1919	465
NORFOLK	7	1919	465
NORFOLK	4	1919	1011
PEARL HARBOR	1	1919	1001
PUGET SOUND	3	1919	926
SOUTH BOSTON	3	1920	1152
PHILADELPHIA	3	1921	1011
CRISTOBAL CZ	1	1933	386
MARE ISLAND	3	1940	693
PEARL HARBOR	2	1941	1000
PHILADELPHIA	4	1941	1092
PUGET SOUND	4	1941	997
PUGET SOUND	5	1941	1030
BAYONNE NJ	7	1942	1092
BOSTON	5	1942	516
LONG BEACH	1	1942	1092
MARE ISLAND	4	1942	435
NEW YORK	5	1942	1092
NEW YORK	6	1942	1092
NORFOLK	8	1942	1092
PEARL HARBOR	3	1942	496
PHILADELPHIA	5	1942	1092
PORTSMOUTH	3	1942	492
SAN DIEGO	1	1942	693
SAN FRANCISCO	4	1942	1092
SAN JUAN PR	1	1942	654
CHARLESTON	3	1943	365
CHARLESTON	4	1943	365
LONG BEACH	2	1943	687
LONG BEACH	3	1943	687
PEARL HARBOR	4	1943	1088
PORTSMOUTH	2	1943	740
SOUTH BOSTON	4	1943	693
BALBOA CZ	3	1944	219
BALBOA CZ	2	1944	424
ROOSEVELT ROADS PR	1	1944	1088
SAN FRANCISCO	5	1944	420
SAN FRANCISCO	6	1944	420
SAN FRANCISCO	7	1944	420
TOTAL	55		

The Cold War drove the building of nine additional graving docks after World War II as listed in Table (5). The 1151 foot long Dry Dock Nr. 6 at Puget Sound Naval shipyard was put into service in 1962. It was designed to accommodate the new classes of aircraft carriers including the nuclear powered *USS ENTERPRISE (CVN 65)*. The other smaller dry docks at Charleston and Mare Island were driven by the construction of the Navy's new nuclear submarine force.

In the late 1980s, the last two graving docks to be built for the United States Navy were the two at the Trident Submarine Refit Facilities at Bangor, Washington and Kings Bay, Georgia. These were self-contained maintenance facilities for the Navy's Ohio Class Fleet Ballistic Submarine force, a key part of the United States' nuclear deterrence.

Table 5 - Nine additional graving docks after World War II.

Location	Dry Dock Number	Date Completed	Length
PHILADELPHIA	1	1956	442
NEW YORK	3	1959	745
PUGET SOUND	6	1962	1151
CHARLESTON	5	1964	751
PUGET SOUND	1	1966	638
CHARLESTON	2	1968	596
MARE ISLAND	1	1968	525
BANGOR TRF	1	1980	700
KINGS BAY TRF	1	1989	700

The total number of graving docks the United States Navy owned in 1968 was 62. This was the high water mark for United States Navy owned and operated graving docks. Soon after, President Nixon's administration closed the Brooklyn, Boston, and Hunter Point Naval Shipyards. The graving docks at Hunters Point came under the cognizance of Mare Island Naval Shipyard until the late 1980s.

Figure (84) is a plot of the number of graving dry docks completed in a particular year. The two spikes in the graph make sense, World War I and World War II.

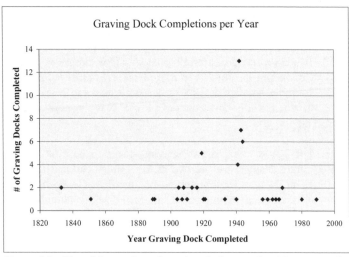

Figure 84 - Plot of the number of graving docks completed in a particular year.

Figure (85) is another plot of the length of the graving dry dock put into service in a year. This plot shows three distinctive graving dock lengths that were built commencing in the late 1800s. The largest were for the battleships and carriers. The intermediate was for the cruisers and destroyers. The smaller dry docks were for the submarines.

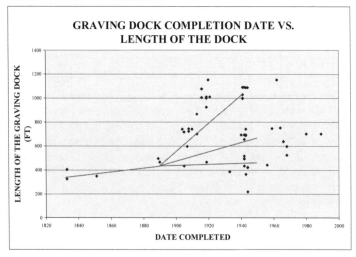

Figure 85 - Length of graving dock versus year completed.

One drydocking I personally conducted at Long Beach Naval Shipyard in the early 1980s was the simultaneous docking of the *USS HOEL (DDG 13) and USS RAMSEY (FFG 2)* in Dry Dock Nr. 1. This was a stern-to-stern double docking at the height of the Cold War while the Reagan Administration was pushing for a 600 ship U.S. Navy.

Double drydockings were required to keep up with the ship repair workload at the time. This allowed other dry dock block buildups to be constructed while work proceeded on these ships. Having another buildup ready to go when these ships undocked allowed other ships and vessels to enter the dry dock on the same water. That meant that the dry dock would not have to be pumped down between drydocking evolutions thus saving the shipyard huge amounts in utility and labor costs.

Even through during the 1980s defense build up under President Reagan, the number of active U.S. Naval shipyards never again reached the levels of the 1960's. No U.S. Naval Shipyards, however, were closed during the Reagan Administration. One of highlights of his Presidency was the activation of the *IOWA* class battleships. Two were activated at Long Beach Naval Shipyard, the *USS NEW JERSEY (BB 62) and USS MISSOURI (BB 63)*. Figure (86) shows the *USS MISSOURI (BB 63)* in Dry Dock Nr. 1 at Long Beach Naval Shipyard in August 1984.

Figure 86 - USS MISSOURI (BB 63) upon entering Dry Dock Nr. 1, Long Beach Naval Shipyard August 1984. (U.S. Navy photo)

With the end of the Cold War during the first Bush Administration, and the subsequent significant downsizing of the United States Armed Forces during the 1990s which concentrated on infrastructure as well as force reduction, four of the remaining eight U.S. Naval Shipyards closed. By the end of the 20th Century only Norfolk, Portsmouth, Puget Sound, and Pearl Harbor Naval Shipyards remained open. The high point of graving docks was 62. By 1999 there were only 22 graving docks under U.S. Navy control and ownership.

From 1793 when President Washington requested the construction of the U.S. Navy's first six frigates to 1968 was 175 years. It took that long to build up to the 62 graving docks and 11 U.S. Naval Shipyards. It took only the last 31 years for the U.S. Navy to divest itself of two-thirds of its graving docks. This reduction was all done in a time period equal to 17 percent of the history of the United States Navy. The last time the U.S. Navy only had only 22 graving docks was 1920. The last time the U.S. Navy only had 4 U.S. Naval shipyards was 1800.

Chapter 20

Other U.S. Navy Ship Drydocking Facilities

Beyond graving and floating dry docks, there are other ways to get U.S. Naval warships out of the water for repair and maintenance. These methods include the use of marine railways, travel lifts, vertical lifts, heavy lift ships, heavy lift floating cranes, and floodable barges. All these methods have been frequently used in the last 20 years. Of all these methods, the U.S. Navy only owns a few marine railways and travel lifts primarily for drydocking yard craft. The other methods are contracted for as needed.

Figure (87) is the view of the marine railway as it was in 1955 at the Washington D.C. Naval Gun Factory, the site of the first marine railway in the United States. Marine railways are used primarily in the smaller private sector yards to dry dock smaller support vessels and yachts. They have been used for the drydocking of naval vessels such as mine counter measure ships and patrol craft. There are no associated ballast tanks or pumps. A winch is required to pull the platform out of the water. The ship is moored over the cradle. As the cradle is hauled up the rail, the ship lands on the cradle and is hauled out of the water with the cradle. To refloat the ship, the cradle is hauled out down the rail until the ship floats off the cradle.

The 1950s brought new and innovative ways to dry dock ships. One of the methods was the vertical lift. One company called SYNCROLIFT©, (now a Rolls Royce Company), invented a vertical lift system in 1954. The vertical lift is a large elevator that can be lowered into the water, have a large vessel positioned over it, and then lift the vessel vertically to the ground level of the shipyard. The first vertical lift SYNCROLIFT developed was built in Miami, Florida, in 1957, and is still operating today.[218]

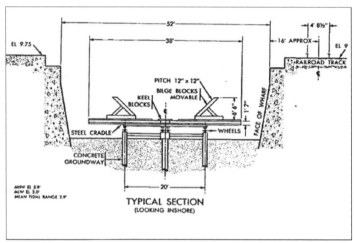

Figure 87 - Marine railway as it was in 1955 at the Washington D.C. Naval Gun Factory.[217] Site of the first marine railway in the United States. (U.S. Navy)

Ships are drydocked on the SYNCROLIFT platform using keel and side blocking systems similar to other forms of drydocking. The blocking system in this case, however, is usually in the form of a steel structure mounted on a system of cars. The docking platform is constructed with a rail system. Once the ships have been raised to ground level, the system of linked cars on which the ship sits is towed off the platform by tractors. This frees up the platform for immediate use for another docking.

In 1984, the largest vertical lift platform in the world was put into operation at what was the Todd Pacific Shipyard at Los Angeles, California. Figure (88) is a photo of the *USS ELLIOTT (DD 967)* as she was being towed off this SYNCROLIFT platform in 1984. This was the largest warship ever drydocked on a SYNCROLIFT at the time. The platform was 656 feet long and 105 feet wide and utilized 110 hoists. Maximum lifting capacity was 20,000 long tons.

I served as a docking observer for this evolution. I was on loan from Long Beach Naval Shipyard to SUPSHIP Long Beach for this evolution.

This docking was challenging, as the *ELLIOTT* required the construction of one of the most difficult drydocking block systems of any surface ship. The side blocks are among the highest of any surface ship. This resulted in a steel transfer car system of considerable size and weight that was capable of handling this 9600 long ton (LT) warship.

Figure 88 - USS ELLIOTT (DD 967) being towed off SYNCROLIFT© at Todd Pacific Shipyard Los Angeles in 1984. (Courtesy SYNCROLIFT)

A key component of the SYNCROLIFT is the use of A.C. synchronous induction motors. These motors operate at one speed regardless of load. Motor speed is a function of the frequency of the A.C. power source. Therefore, any number of identical motors operating from the same power source will behave as if mechanically linked. Another key component is the articulated platform. This platform distributes hull loads to each lift point.

In the case of the *ELLIOTT* docking, I witnessed the first accurate weighing and load distribution measurement of a *SPRUANCE* class destroyer. The load limit per linear foot was the limiting factor during this docking.

The lifting hoists are positioned along each side of the platform. Each hoist supports one end of a main transverse beam by wire rope reaved through sheaves mounted on the beam and at the hoist. The hoists are driven by an AC synchronous induction motor through a gearbox that drives a bull gear, which is integral to the wire rope drum. The drums are grooved to accept the full length of wire rope, so only a single layer of rope is wrapped on the drum. Load cells and current relays shut down all of the motors before motor slip can occur. There is also a mechanical ratchet system to provide a safety locking mechanism as the ship is raised. It is the motor type and single layer of rope that results in the synchronization of platform movement.[219]

A SYNCROLIFT rating is based on the lifting capacity per unit length. The maximum load on each keel block must be determined based on the vessel's load distribution. This was near the maximum in the case of the *ELLIOTT* docking. The current maximum lifting capacity of a SYNCROLIFT is over 25,000 long tons.

The platform can be raised at a rate of 0.2 and 0.5 meters per second. This relatively quick speed is advantageous during drydockings of damaged vessels. The *USS BARBOUR COUNTY (LST 1195)* was docked at the Todd Los Angeles SYNCROLIFT in a severely damaged condition. This ship had gone aground on the beach at Coronado, California for a couple days and suffered considerable hull damage. Free communication (flooding) was occurring between the sea and her fuel/ballast tanks even as the ship was raised out of the water in the SYNCROLIFT. I was the docking observer for this evolution as well.

When the *BARBOUR COUNTY* was lifted out of the water by the platform, water was pouring profusely out of the starboard tanks. It became impossible to stop the discharge of water, and this would have prevented a safe docking in a floating dry dock. In the case of the SYNCROLIFT, with its inherently stable configuration and docking speed, the ship could be raised and removed from the platform without overloading any of the blocking system or causing an instability situation. It should be noted that for this evolution, double the normal side blocks were used in the blocking system due to the uneven (not per drawing) shape of the hull. The hull shape had become "hungry horsed" where there were significant indentations between frames in the hull plating. Additional side blocks was easily added to the blocking car system.

The SYNCROLIFT system utilizes a computer added control system called Advanced Technology Loading Articulated Shiplifts (ATLAS). This system analyzes the load taken by each hoist and actually determines the docked vessel's longitudinal center of gravity (LCG). In addition, the system also monitors the differential loads between the port and starboard hoists. This feature enables the system to determine any potentially dangerous off centerline loads on the docked vessel and virtually eliminates the possibility of a sudden list developing on a ship when undocking. This sometimes happens in graving docks, when major changes occur during the docking period and inaccurate weight changes are recorded.

In the case of the *BARBOUR COUNTY*, the flooding load conditions were safely monitored throughout the docking evolution. It was, also, possible to be completely assured of a stable condition after the ship was repaired and placed back on the platform for the undocking evolution that occurred months later.

Being able to accurately measure the longitudinal center of gravity while on the platform, enables the naval architect to accurately update ship information books after major refit periods where large weight changes have occurred. This is especially useful where conversions have occurred that significantly change the underbody shape of the ship. The actual load distribution measurements help validate all predictions. Another interesting curve can be generated using the SYNCROLIFT ATLAS system. That curve is the Tons Per Inch Immersion. Even before a ship becomes buoyant enough to float off the lowering platform, as soon as the hull begins to be immersed, buoyancy forces start acting on the ship's hull. ATLAS can measure these forces, as the load cells will detect the decreasing load on the hoists as the platform continues to be lowered.

Having these known loads inherently leads to safer docking evolutions. In a graving dock, where load distribution is calculated but not measured, many ships have been floated off blocks and have immediately taken extreme lists to one side or another. If not capsizing completely (which has happened), the ship can experience significant hull damage by striking one set of side blocks. The SYNCROLIFT virtually eliminates this as a possibility as off center loads are measured prior to the ship being immersed in water where the buoyancy forces start acting on the hull.

Another advantage to being able to accurately weigh a ship after a major refit or after initial construction is to determine the actual displacement of a ship. Most military new construction or conversion contracts place strict ship displacement and stability requirements on the shipbuilder. If these limits are violated, stiff financial penalties occur. Not only can the ship be weighed while on the platform, but also since the entire ship system is on cars, these cars can be fitted with load cells at almost any time.

SYNCROLIFT offers many advantages to the docking process. It is actually a transportable docking asset to a degree. The SYNCROLIFT shown in Figure (89) on which *USS ELLIOTT* docked at Todd Los Angeles, which was the largest SYNCROLIFT in the world, was moved to Malaysia Shipyard & Engineering in Johore, Malaysia. This entire SYNCROLIFT was reconfigured and is again one of the largest vertical lifts in the world.[220]

Figure 89 - Largest SYNCROLIFT in the world in Los Angeles 1984. Was moved to Malaysia in 1997. (Courtesy SYNCROLIFT, Inc.)

Chapter 21

New Innovations in Ship Transport and Repair

The heavy lift ship is another relatively new method of getting ships out the water. It has the ability to transport ships, oilrigs, cranes, or submarines up to 14 knots anywhere in the world. Figure (90) shows the heavy lift ship, *SUPER SERVANT 3*, leaving Little Creek, Virginia, Naval Amphibious Base transporting three U.S. Navy MSO's and one Mine Countermeasure Ship to the Arabian Gulf August 29, 1990 in support of Operation Desert Shield. This method of docking and transport was necessary due to the Iraqi invasion of Kuwait. I was the docking officer for the onload at Little Creek, Virginia and offload at Bahrain.

These ships [*USS ADROIT (MSO 509)*, *USS LEADER (MSO 490)*, *USS IMPERVIOUS (MSO 449)*, and *USS AVENGER (MCM 1)*] on the heavy lift, arrived 31 days later off Bahrain. They were immediately offloaded and were ready for service literally at the edge of an active minefield. The ships arrived with engines overhauled, fresh crews flown in, full tanks of fresh water, full fuel tanks, full water tanks, freezers and chill boxes full of food and all magazines full of ammunition. During the transit, underwater hull work was also accomplished including sea valve repair, propeller repairs, sea growth removal, hull painting, and transducer repairs.

These types of heavy lift ships need about 50 feet of water to onload cargo of this type. They have enormous flexibility and can carry large cargo such as oilrigs from shipyards and deliver them to their jack-up sites in oil fields around the world. The U.S. Navy has not only used these ships over seven times for mine countermeasure ship transports, but also for damaged ship transports such as the *USS SAMUEL B. ROBERTS (FFG 58)* after she was heavily damaged by a mine in the Arabian Gulf April 14, 1988. After being attacked by terrorists in October 2000, the *USS COLE (DDG 67)* was transported back from off of Yemen. She was heavy lifted directly to her building yard, Ingalls Shipbuilding and was off loaded after a patch was placed on the hull damage in December 2001.

Figure 90 - SUPER SERVANT 3 with three MSO's and one MCM leaving Little Creek Naval Amphibious Base August 29, 1990 underway to the Arabian Gulf. (Photo by Richard D. Hepburn)

These heavy lift ships can berth a caretaker crew as well as miscellaneous cargo in standard containers. They provide electrical power, firemain, and fresh water to the ships on the cargo deck. Many navies around the world have used this method to transport warships and submarines especially for foreign sales of ships. Recently the *HMS NOTTINGHAM* was heavylifted back from Australia to the U.K. after she ran hard aground.

In 1996, with the closing of Long Beach Naval Shipyard, the heavy lift ship *SEA SWAN* was used to transport the Nazi war prize crane *TITAN (YD-171)* from the shipyard to the Panama Canal for use there in lock repair.[221] The *SEA SWAN* was converted into a heavy lift ship. It has a deeper draft, and therefore, requires deeper water for ballasting down and loading cargo on its cargo deck.

Another method of drydocking and transport is the use of floodable barges. Figure (91) shows the *USS OSPREY (MHC 51)* underway in the Chesapeake Bay on a barge being towed to the Aberdeen Proving Grounds. The ship was later transferred from the barge onto a marine railway where it was lowered into a lake for shock testing. Floodable barges can be used in a couple of ways. They can be ballasted down and basically sunk with only guideposts and trunks left exposed to pump out the barge. A vessel to be drydocked is then maneuvered over the barge, aligned to the guideposts, and the barge is pumped out and the vessel lands on the barge blocking system.

Figure 91 - USS OSPREY (MHC 51) on a floodable barge being transported in Chesapeake Bay to Aberdeen Proving Grounds for shock testing. (Photo courtesy Jim Sandison)

The other approach, as was used in the case of the *USS OSPREY*, has the barge move into a graving dock and land on the blocks. The barge is flooded and the graving dock is then flooded and the vessel to be placed on the barge is then brought into the graving dock and when the graving dock is pumped out, the vessel lands on a blocking system on top of the barge. The barge is then pumped out, and the graving dock is then flooded, and the barge and vessel float off and are removed from the dock. Figure (92) shows the *USS OSPREY* landed on a barge in a graving dock at Norfolk Naval Shipyard.

A rail track on top of the barge was used to pull *OSPREY* off the barge at Aberdeen. This evolution was unique in that it used three different drydocking methods all in one evolution. A graving dock, floodable barge, and marine railway were all used to get

OSPREY in and out of the shock test lake (basin) at Aberdeen. This historic event allowed the shock test to occur in a test basin, avoiding numerous environmental restrictions present when the open ocean is used for shock testing.

Figure 92 - USS OSPREY (MHC 51) on a floodable barge, in a graving dock at Norfolk Naval Shipyard. (courtesy of Jim Sandison).

This method of using a floodable barge in conjunction with another dry dock has been employed for decades. I used this method in 1982 to offload a submarine shock test vehicle off a floodable barge and to later reload the vehicle back on this floodable barge at Long Beach Naval Shipyard. The offload evolution took 35 hours. A section of a 688-class submarine was loaded on a barge via crane at Newport News Shipbuilding and Dry Dock Company in Virginia. This assembly was towed via the Panama Canal to Long Beach Naval Shipyard where it was put into Dry Dock Nr. 2. The dry dock was dewatered and the barge was then filled with water. When the dry dock was flooded, the vehicle floated off the barge. Once the vehicle was removed from the dry dock, the dry dock was again pumped out. The barge was dewatered, then the dry dock was again flooded and the barge floated and was removed from the dry dock. To put the vehicle back on the barge, the opposite method was used.

Chapter 22

A 21ST Century Need Lives on for This Age Old Process

From Commodore Rodgers' marine railway at the Washington Navy Yard in 1822, to the exotic methods of heavy lift ships, vertical lifts, and floodable barges, the ability to dry dock warships, when needed, has been key to the success of United States Navy's operations. Several times in American history, the availability of a dry dock was key to the success of a subsequent naval battle.

The potential problem facing the Navy is the future accessing of sufficient repair facilities to handle repairs in the event of future increased demand. Even with the more exotic ways of lifting ships out of water, the locations for drydocking have been drastically reduced. Tables (6) and (7) are estimates of the U.S. Navy owned graving and floating dry docks still in operation as of June 1999.

Table 6 - Estimates of the U.S. Navy owned graving docks still in operation as of June 1999

FACILITY	GRAVING DOCKS
Norfolk Naval Shipyard	8
Pearl Harbor Naval Shipyard	4
Portsmouth Naval Shipyard	3
Puget Sound Naval Shipyard	5
Trident Refit Facility, Bangor, WA	1
Trident Refit Facility, Kings Bay, GA	1
San Diego Naval Station	1
TOTAL	23

Table 7 - Estimates of the U.S. Navy owned floating dry docks still in operation as of June 1999

CLASS OF FLOATING DRY DOCK	APPROXIMATE NUMBER
AFDB	0
AFDM	1
AFDL	0
ARD	1
YFD	1
TOTAL	3

From 1968 to 1999, there was a drop from 62 to 23 graving docks owned and operated by the U.S. Navy. Figure (93) plots this data. This represents a 63 % reduction of graving dock U.S. Navy owned capacity in 31 years.

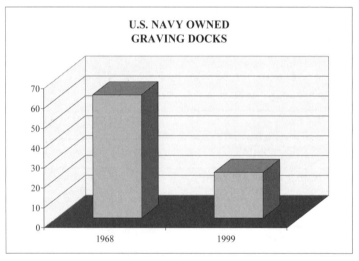

Figure 93 - Change in number of U.S. Navy graving docks since 1968.

From 1955 to 2003, there was been a corresponding reduction in the number of U.S. Navy warships of 67%. Table (8) lists the changes in numbers of each class of warship.[222]

Table 8 - Reduction iN numbers of U.S. Naval warships from 1955 to 2003.

SHIP CLASS	1955	2003	% CHANGE
Submarines	142	54	-62%
Attack Carriers	16	12	-25%
Surface Combatants	329	112	-66%
Amphibious	175	40	-77%
TOTAL	**662**	**218**	**-67%**

Therefore, one could conclude, that since warship and graving dock reductions both reduced in similar relative amounts, this phenomenon is intuitively acceptable. However, if the U.S. Navy, again increases its number of warships or repair requirements due to battle damage, the permanent loss of these graving docks may prove a formidable problem as waterfront property is consumed for other uses and the cost of reconstruction exceeds budget resources. Floating dry docks could be readily built or purchased. However, their use has limitations. In the case of these floating dry docks, the challenge is finding deep enough water in a safe harbor suitable for drydocking operations. Environmental laws against dredging make this process complex, expensive and time consuming.

The private sector's loss in capacity also contributes to the Navy's predicament. The problem facing the largest six private sector shipyards in the United States — now owned by only two corporations — is the need to sustain an industry capable of building the number of warships the Navy might need in the future. All heavy lift ships are foreign owned. The *COLE's* heavy lift to the United States happened expeditiously. However this was only due to the chance location of an available foreign heavy lift ship in the region. Figure (94) shows *USS COLE (DDG 67)* on heavy lift ship *M/V BLUE MARLIN* upon arrival at Ingalls Shipbuilding in Pascagoula, Mississippi December 13, 2000.

At the moment, the Navy is not generating enough business to assure that all private yards survive. The 1997 Quadrennial Defense Review (QDR), while retaining 12 carrier battlegroups and 12 amphibious readiness groups, called for the number of surface combatants in the fleet to be reduced from 128 to 116.[223] Since 1992, the number of Navy ships under construction dropped from 135 to 39 and is predicted to drop to the low 20's over the next five years.[224] In January 2000, the Future Year Defense Program (FYDP) for Ship Construction Navy (SCN) was nothing short of disaster for the surface Navy with the stretch out of the DDG 51 construction from 3 to 2 ships a year split between 2 yards and the continued delays of the LPD program. The DD21 program looked tenuous in early 2001 and was completely changed in 2002 to the DDX program with an associated delay in production schedules and additional uncertainties in the shipyards.

Figure 94 - Arrival of USS COLE (DDG 67) on heavy lift ship M/V BLUE MARLIN at Pascagoula, Mississippi, December 13, 2000. (U.S. Navy Photo)

The United Kingdom's Ministry of Defense (MOD) is similarly plagued by the effects of the end of the Cold War and reduced defense budgets. The dockyards at Portsmouth and Devonport as well as all their other government operated dockyards were turned over to the private sector to operate in the late 1990s although the MOD retains ownership of the facilities. This is called Government Owned and Contractor Operated (GOCO).

The United States has not yet taken this path with the Navy operated Naval Shipyards. Some of the closed naval shipyards are owned by the local governments and they lease the dry docks to private shipyards such as Deytens Shipyard. Deytens utilizes some of the graving docks at what was the Charleston Naval Shipyard in South Carolina. Deytens Shipyard is very active in executing the U.S. Navy's foreign military sales contract. It refurbishes warships being sold to foreign navies.

On the West Coast, the ex Hunters Point Naval Shipyard Dry Dock Nr. 4 is being used by a private contractor to scrap U.S. Navy ships as shown in Figure (95). As these docks are filled with scrap, it makes these docks unavailable for urgent repairs. These graving docks are also no longer certified by the Naval Sea Systems Command's Dry Dock Safety and Certification program for warship drydockings.

Figure 95 - The Ex Hunters Point Naval Shipyard Dry Dock #4 in 1999 with ship scrapping in progress. (U.S. Navy Photo)

In June 1999, there was some hope for retaining part of the closed Long Beach Naval Shipyard as a marine construction and repair facility. Some of the shops and the large dry dock, Dry Dock Nr. 1, would be used for the construction of utility barges. However this did not materialize and the entire ex-shipyard and what was the adjacent naval station is being completely converted to a container port. All of the three graving docks at Long Beach have been or are in the process of being filled in as of April 2003.[225]

Chapter 23

- Conclusion -
A Maritime Nation Need to Remain Aware of Her Required Maritime Capacity

For the U.S. Navy to retain a production stream for new warships and a viable number of sites to repair ships in the future, a wary eye must be kept on the overall United States shipyard capacity. Any markets for private sector United States shipyards are good news for the U.S. Navy. Such markets are, however, very volatile, with fierce worldwide competition and foreign government subsidies. For instance, foreign subsidized yards have captured the cruise line ship production market. The state owned Fincantieri Shipyards of Italy have experienced a financial turnaround with a 40 plus percent market share in the cruise ship construction business. The float-out in May 1997 of the 85,000 gross ton *DISNEY MAGIC* was a cornerstone of recent achievements by this world class Italian shipbuilder.[226]

The upsurge in the Gulf Coast marine industry in the late 1990s due to the offshore drilling market offered promise in keeping the U.S. marine industry alive along with recent increases in containership and other private sector construction contracts at U. S. yards. Other innovative approaches need to be considered to keep the marine industry current in warship engineering. This could include a whole new type of "bumper to bumper" ship maintenance contracts that would replace or compliment uniformed and civilian U.S. Naval personnel for complete classes of ships.

There is no escaping the worldwide interests of the United States. This inescapable fact requires a maritime force necessary to protect trade, project the interests of the United States, and maintain security on our own shores. To do this, the American people must decide that the United States Navy is here to stay, long term, and there will always be a requirement for modern shore facilities to construct and repair warships.

New facilities will indeed be required as evidenced by the "beyond PANAMAX" cruise ships such as the Royal Caribbean *EAGLE* Class and Carnival *DESTINY* class. These ships could only be drydocked in one commercial yard on the East Coast. That is at the Northrop Grumman Newport News Shipyard, Newport News, Virginia. However, most of their dry docks are busy with construction and repair of aircraft carriers. Beyond PANAMAX means too larg for the Panama Canal.

Because of the lack of available drydocking and repair facilities adequate to service these huge cruise ships, a European country put a drydocking facility in the Bahamas. This happened recently when the floating dry dock at Cascade General was towed from Portland, Oregon to the Bahamas.

These beyond PANAMAX ships almost exclusively stay in the Caribbean for their cruise runs. If these ships cannot come to the United States for drydocking, a huge business opportunity will be lost as well as an opportunity for the United States Navy to have other customers share the cost of dry dock maintenance and operations.

> "The size of the Eagle Class ships (311m x 48m) [1020.3 ft x 157.48 ft] presents [Royal Caribbean International] RCI with a problem – where to carry out future drydocking schedules of the vessels. The vessels are all intended for the Caribbean service out of Miami and therefore would be expected to be dry docked on the U.S. East or Gulf Coasts. However, due to size factors, there are very few facilities available in those areas..."[227]

American naval dry docks, however, have reached an apex in their history and are now well on the ebbing side, as graving docks continue to be abandoned and floating dry docks are no longer constructed in this country. The need persists, but the vision is not yet set for the potential direction ahead. A nation rich in maritime history and having an obvious future reliance on maritime trade and protection must set a new course to avoid the shoal that grounded ancient maritime powers.

The abandonment of seven U.S. Navy owned prime waterfront locations for ship repair is forever lost to the American people who hold their Navy almost for granted. They assume it is there, always ready to answer the Country's call when needed. Losing this waterfront property, is not like abandoning a shipyard in 1900. Now, immediately on the wake of the Shipyard Commanders locking the gate for the last time; developers follow close behind with bulldozers to fill in dry docks and create container ports or housing or commercial properties.

Another round of BRAC (Base Realignment and Closure) is being discussed by the Department of Defense. Among those candidate bases may be the Portsmouth Naval Shipyard. If this occurs, the number of U.S. Navy owned shipyards and dry docks would be down to those at Norfolk, Puget Sound, and Pearl Harbor.

Meanwhile, the few private sector shipyards are modernizing. Bath Iron Works, A General Dynamics Company, launched its last ship using inclined building ways in June 2001. Ship erection and launching is now completed via their new Land Level Transfer Facility (LLTF) and new floating dry dock. This 14-acre facility greatly increased ship construction efficiency and capacity. This was a financial necessity, yet bold step by General Dynamics, and should be seen by the U.S. Government as vital to the U.S. national interests.

Floating dry docks should be considered as well as national interests before more are lost to overseas competitors. The following was written by Mark Helprin and appeared in the Wall Street Journal April 24, 2001:

> "What remains of the order of battle is crippled by a lack of the unglamorous, costly supports that are the first to go when there isn't enough money. Consider the floating dry dock. By putting ships back into action with minimal transit time, floating dry docks are force preservers and multipliers. In 1972, the United States had 94. Now it has 14. Though history is bitter and clear, this kind of mistake persists."[228]

What does this mean to the future of the United States Navy having so few graving docks and floating docks at their immediate disposal? It is hard to imagine this not being a profound weakness. The question is how to fix it. Figure (96), shows the disappearance of what was the Long Beach Navy Yard and conversion into a container port. With this conversion still happening, the solution will not be easy.

The United States just concluded the hot phase of its war in Iraq in April 2003. This followed on the heels of the unprovoked terrorist attacks of September 11, 2001. During the Iraq war in April 2003, 72% of the Navy's ships were underway at one time. If there had been any other crises occur in the world, which almost happened in North Korea, the number of Navy ships available would have been inadequate. The Navy is now professing the need for more surface combatants (from 116 to 160) and desires to increase the size of the Navy from 300 ships to 375 ships.[229]

More ships mean an inevitable need for more dry docks. It always has been this way and it always will be as long as underwater maintenance is required. That work, though reduced, is still significant and vital for reliable and efficient ship operations. The American people expect excellence and victory from their Navy. The Navy will need her dry docks to succeed in its future endeavors. Planning now for that need is essential.

Figure 96 - Ex Long Beach Naval Shipyard and Naval Station on October 7, 2002. Two of three dry docks have been filled in at the shipyard as the entire complex was turned into a container port. (Photo by Debra A. Hepburn).

References

[1] MacDougall, Philip, Ph.D., "The Royal Dockyards, The Naval Dockyards Society Website, http://www.canterbury.u-net.com/Dockyards/page3.html, United Kingdom, 1997.

[2] Flagship Portsmouth, "History of Innovation", http://www.compulink.co.uk/~flagship/Frames.htm , Portsmouth, UK, 1997.

[3] http://www.ville-rochefort.fr/ville/hermione/her105.htm

[4] Jarvis, Harry R., *Transactions of the North-East Coast Institution of Engineers and Shipbuilders*, Newcastle-Upon-Tyne and London, Andrew Reid & Company, Limited, Printers and Publishers, 10 January 1908.

[5] Cook, Volney E. & Paul S. Crandall, "General Discussion of Floating Dry docks", *Transactions*, Society of Naval Architects and Marine Engineers, New York, November 1957, pp. 289 & 303.

[6] Flagship Portsmouth, "History of Innovation", http://www.compulink.co.uk/~flagship/Frames.htm , Portsmouth, UK, 1997.

[7] www.nnsy1.navy.mil/NNSYHIST.HTM; Norfolk Naval Shipyard Website, 1998.

[8] Butt, Marshall W.; *Portsmouth Under Four Flags*; Portsmouth Historical Association; 1971

[9] www.nnsy1.navy.mil/NNSYHIST.HTM;Norfolk Naval Shipyard Website, 1998.

[10] www.nnsy1.navy.mil/NNSYHIST.HTM;Norfolk Naval Shipyard Website, 1998.

[11] http://members.tripod.com/~ntgen/bw/loammi.html, Norris Taylor, 2000.

[12] Sprout, Harold and Margaret, *The Rise of American Naval Power 1776-1918*, Naval Institute Press, Annapolis, MD, 1966, pp. 55-56.

[13] Sweetman, Jack, *American Naval History*, Naval Institute Press, Annapolis, MD, 1991, pp. 16.

[14] http://www.nnsy1.navy.mil/History/HISTORY.HTM, Norfolk Naval Shipyard Website, 1998.

[15] http://members.xoom.com/ex_Yardbird/, Philadelphia Naval Shipyard ex-Yard Bird website, 1998.

[16] Labaree, Benjamin W.; William M. Fowler, Jr.; Edward W. Sloan; John B. Hattendorf; Jeffery J. Safford; Andrew W. German; America and the Sea: A Maritime History; Mystic Seaport; 1998; pp. 184.

[17] Sweetman, Jack, *American Naval History*, Naval Institute Press, Annapolis, MD, 1991, pp. 17-19.

[18] http://members.xoom.com/ex_Yardbird/, Philadelphia Naval Shipyard ex-Yard Bird website, 1998.
[19] http://www.nnsy1.navy.mil/History/HISTORY.HTM, Norfolk Naval Shipyard Website, 1998.
[20] www.nps.gov/bost/cnyintro.htm ,National Park Service website, 1998
[21] http://www.nnsy1.navy.mil/History/HISTORY.HTM, Norfolk Naval Shipyard Website, 1998.
[22] Potter, E.B., *Sea Power, A Naval History*, Naval Institute Press, Annapolis, MD, 1981, pp. 89.
[23] Stuart, Charles B.; *The Naval Dry Docks of the United States, Fourth Edition, Part Second, Floating Dry Docks*; D. Van Nostrand; New York, New York; 1870; pp. 8-9.
[24] Ibid.
[25] Sweetman, Jack, *American Naval History*, Naval Institute Press, Annapolis, MD, 1991, pp. 35.
[26] Pike, John; http://www.fas.org/man/dod-101/company/shipyard/portsmouth.htm; July 14, 1998.
[27] www.NAVSEA.navy.mil/NNSYHIST.HTM; Norfolk Naval Shipyard Website, 1998.
[28] Pike, John ; http://www.fas.org/man/dod-101/company/shipyard/new_york.htm; March 06, 1999.
[29] "Washington Navy Historic Landmark Points of Interest", U.S. Government Printing office, 1991.
[30] Stuart, Charles B.; *The Naval Dry Docks of the United States, Fourth Edition, Part Second, Floating Dry Docks*; D. Van Nostrand; New York, New York; 1870; pp. 10.
[31] Stuart, Charles B.; *The Naval Dry Docks of the United States, Fourth Edition, Part Second, Floating Dry Docks*; D. Van Nostrand; New York, New York; 1870; pp. 10.
[32] Cook, Volney E., "General Discussion of Floating Dry docks", *Transactions*, The Society of Naval Architects and Marine Engineers, November 1957, pp. 289.
[33] The Funk & Wagnalls New Encyclopedia, 1995.
[34] Ibid.
[35] Ibid.
[36] "Washington Navy Historic Landmark Points of Interest", U.S. Government Printing office, 1991.
[37] http://www.nnsy1.navy.mil/History/HISTORY.HTM, Norfolk Naval Shipyard Website, 1998.
[39] Ibid.
[40] Schodek, Daniel L.; Landmarks in American Civil Engineering; MIT Press; Cambridge, Massachusetts; 1987; pp. 340.

[41] Schodek, Daniel L.; Landmarks in American Civil Engineering; MIT Press; Cambridge, Massachusetts; 1987; pp. 340.
[42] Ibid.
[43] "American Ships of the Line", Naval History Division, Navy Department, Washington, D.C. 1969.
[44] Norfolk Naval Shipyard, "Dry docks Docking Data", 1951, courtesy of Portsmouth Naval Shipyard Museum.
[45] Butt, Marshall W.; *Portsmouth Under Four Flags*; Portsmouth Historical Association; 1971.
[46] Miller, Nathan, *The U.S. NAVY, An Illustrated History*, American Heritage Publishing Company, Inc., New York, and the United States Naval Institute Press, Annapolis, Maryland, 1977, pp. 107.
[47] Stuart, Charles B.; *The Naval Dry Docks of the United States, Fourth Edition*; D. Van Nostrand; New York, New York; 1870; pp. 66.
[48] Schodek, Daniel L., *Landmarks in American Civil Engineering*, MIT Press, Cambridge, Massachusetts, 1987, pp. 339.
[49] Bruff, J.G.; Copy of Lithograph from a sketch on stone, "American Ships of the Line", Naval History Division, Navy Department, Washington, D.C. 1969.
[50] "American Ships of the Line", Naval History Division, Navy Department, Washington, D.C. 1969.
[51] Department of the Navy, http://www.nnsy1.navy.mil/History/HISTORY.HTM, Norfolk Naval Shipyard Website, 1998.
[52] Bruff, J.G.; Copy of Lithograph from a sketch on stone, "American Ships of the Line", Naval History Division, Navy Department, Washington, D.C. 1969.
[53] Greenhill, Ralph; Engineer's Witness; David R. Godine, Publisher; The Coach House Press; Boston; 1985; pp. 24, *Sketch of the Civil Engineering of North America*, London, 1838, p. 29 .
[54] *Sketch of the Civil Engineering of North America*, London, 1838, p. 28
[55] Stuart, Charles B.; *The Naval Dry Docks of the United States, Fourth Edition*; D. Van Norstrand; New York, NY; 1870; pp. 14.
[56] http://members.xoom.com/ex_Yardbird/, Philadelphia Naval Shipyard Yard Bird website, 1998.
[57] Stuart, Charles B.; *The Naval Dry Docks of the United States, Fourth Edition*; D. Van Norstrand; New York, NY; 1870.
[58] Stuart, Charles B.; *The Naval Dry Docks of the United States, Fourth Edition*; D. Van Norstrand; New York, NY; 1870.
[59] Stuart, Charles B.*; The Naval Dry Docks of the United States;* D.

Van Norstrand ; New York, NY; 1852; pp. 11.

[60] Greenhill, Ralph, *Engineer's Witness,* The Coach House Press, Toronto, David R. Godine, Publisher, Boston, 1985, p. 24.

[61] Stuart, Charles B.; *The Naval Dry Docks of the United States, Fourth Edition*; D. Van Norstrand; New York, NY; 1870; pp. 71.

[62] Stuart, Charles B.; *The Naval Dry Docks of the United States, Fourth Edition*; D. Van Norstrand; New York, NY; 1870; pp. 69.

[63] Stuart, Charles B.; *The Naval Dry Docks of the United States, Fourth Edition*; D. Van Norstrand; New York, NY; 1870; pp. 78.

[64] Department of the Navy Naval Facilities Engineering Command, *Drydocking Facilities Design Manual*, June 1969, pp. 29-11-71.

[65] Stuart, Charles B.; *The Naval Dry Docks of the United States, Fourth Edition*; D. Van Norstrand; New York, NY; 1870; pp. 70.

[66] Stuart, Charles B.; *The Naval Dry Docks of the United States, Fourth Edition*; D. Van Norstrand; New York, NY; 1870; pp. 12.

[67] Sprout, Harold & Margaret; *The Rise of American Naval Power 1776-1918*; Naval Institute Press, Annapolis, MD, 1939, pp. 137.

[68] Sweetman, Jack, *American Naval History*, Naval Institute Press, Annapolis, MD, 1991, pp. 45-58.

[69] Portsmouth Naval Shipyard, "Cradle of American Shipbuilding", December 1978.

[70] Ibid.

[71] http://www.nnsy1.navy.mil/History/HISTORY.HTM, Norfolk Naval Shipyard Website, 1998.

[72] Cook, Volney E., "General Discussion of Floating Dry docks", *Transactions*, The Society of Naval Architects and Marine Engineers, November 1957, pp. 290.

[73] Portsmouth Naval Shipyard, "Cradle of American Shipbuilding", December 1978.

[74] Ibid.

[75] Lott, Arnold S., LCDR, USN; *A Long Line of Ships, Mare Island's Century of Naval Activity in California*, United States Naval Institute, Annapolis, MD, 1954, pp. 21-23.

[76] White, Theodore D.; *An Outline of Shipbuilding Theoretical and Practical*; John Wiley & Son; New York; 1873; pp. 309-310.

[77] White, Theodore D.; *An Outline of Shipbuilding Theoretical and Practical*; John Wiley & Son; New York; 1873; pp. 310.

[78] Lott, Arnold S., LCDR, USN; *A Long Line of Ships, Mare Island's Century of Naval Activity in California*, United States Naval Institute, Annapolis, MD, 1954, pp. 14.

[79] Lott, Arnold S., LCDR, USN; *A Long Line of Ships, Mare Island's Century of Naval Activity in California*, United States Naval Institute, Annapolis, MD, 1954, pp. 21-23.

[60] Greenhill, Ralph, *Engineer's Witness,* The Coach House Press, Toronto, David R. Godine, Publisher, Boston, 1985, p. 24.

[61] Stuart, Charles B.; *The Naval Dry Docks of the United States, Fourth Edition*; D. Van Norstrand; New York, NY; 1870; pp. 71.

[62] Stuart, Charles B.; *The Naval Dry Docks of the United States, Fourth Edition*; D. Van Norstrand; New York, NY; 1870; pp. 69.

[63] Stuart, Charles B.; *The Naval Dry Docks of the United States, Fourth Edition*; D. Van Norstrand; New York, NY; 1870; pp. 78.

[64] Department of the Navy Naval Facilities Engineering Command, *Drydocking Facilities Design Manual*, June 1969, pp. 29-11-71.

[65] Stuart, Charles B.; *The Naval Dry Docks of the United States, Fourth Edition*; D. Van Norstrand; New York, NY; 1870; pp. 70.

[66] Stuart, Charles B.; *The Naval Dry Docks of the United States, Fourth Edition*; D. Van Norstrand; New York, NY; 1870; pp. 12.

[67] Sprout, Harold & Margaret; *The Rise of American Naval Power 1776-1918*; Naval Institute Press, Annapolis, MD, 1939, pp. 137.

[68] Sweetman, Jack, *American Naval History*, Naval Institute Press, Annapolis, MD, 1991, pp. 45-58.

[69] Portsmouth Naval Shipyard, "Cradle of American Shipbuilding", December 1978.

[70] Ibid.

[71] http://www.nnsy1.navy.mil/History/HISTORY.HTM, Norfolk Naval Shipyard Website, 1998.

[72] Cook, Volney E., "General Discussion of Floating Dry docks", *Transactions*, The Society of Naval Architects and Marine Engineers, November 1957, pp. 290.

[73] Portsmouth Naval Shipyard, "Cradle of American Shipbuilding", December 1978.

[74] Ibid.

[75] Lott, Arnold S., LCDR, USN; *A Long Line of Ships, Mare Island's Century of Naval Activity in California*, United States Naval Institute, Annapolis, MD, 1954, pp. 21-23.

[76] White, Theodore D.; *An Outline of Shipbuilding Theoretical and Practical*; John Wiley & Son; New York; 1873; pp. 309-310.

[77] White, Theodore D.; *An Outline of Shipbuilding Theoretical and Practical*; John Wiley & Son; New York; 1873; pp. 310.

[78] Lott, Arnold S., LCDR, USN; *A Long Line of Ships, Mare Island's Century of Naval Activity in California*, United States Naval Institute, Annapolis, MD, 1954, pp. 14.

[79] Lott, Arnold S., LCDR, USN; *A Long Line of Ships, Mare Island's Century of Naval Activity in California*, United States Naval Institute, Annapolis, MD, 1954, pp. 21-23.

[60] Greenhill, Ralph, *Engineer's Witness,* The Coach House Press, Toronto, David R. Godine, Publisher, Boston, 1985, p. 24.

[61] Stuart, Charles B.; *The Naval Dry Docks of the United States, Fourth Edition*; D. Van Norstrand; New York, NY; 1870; pp. 71.

[62] Stuart, Charles B.; *The Naval Dry Docks of the United States, Fourth Edition*; D. Van Norstrand; New York, NY; 1870; pp. 69.

[63] Stuart, Charles B.; *The Naval Dry Docks of the United States, Fourth Edition*; D. Van Norstrand; New York, NY; 1870; pp. 78.

[64] Department of the Navy Naval Facilities Engineering Command, *Drydocking Facilities Design Manual*, June 1969, pp. 29-11-71.

[65] Stuart, Charles B.; *The Naval Dry Docks of the United States, Fourth Edition*; D. Van Norstrand; New York, NY; 1870; pp. 70.

[66] Stuart, Charles B.; *The Naval Dry Docks of the United States, Fourth Edition*; D. Van Norstrand; New York, NY; 1870; pp. 12.

[67] Sprout, Harold & Margaret; *The Rise of American Naval Power 1776-1918*; Naval Institute Press, Annapolis, MD, 1939, pp. 137.

[68] Sweetman, Jack, *American Naval History*, Naval Institute Press, Annapolis, MD, 1991, pp. 45-58.

[69] Portsmouth Naval Shipyard, "Cradle of American Shipbuilding", December 1978.

[70] Ibid.

[71] http://www.nnsy1.navy.mil/History/HISTORY.HTM, Norfolk Naval Shipyard Website, 1998.

[72] Cook, Volney E., "General Discussion of Floating Dry docks", *Transactions*, The Society of Naval Architects and Marine Engineers, November 1957, pp. 290.

[73] Portsmouth Naval Shipyard, "Cradle of American Shipbuilding", December 1978.

[74] Ibid.
[75] Lott, Arnold S., LCDR, USN; *A Long Line of Ships, Mare Island's Century of Naval Activity in California*, United States Naval Institute, Annapolis, MD, 1954, pp. 21-23.
[76] White, Theodore D.; *An Outline of Shipbuilding Theoretical and Practical*; John Wiley & Son; New York; 1873; pp. 309-310.
[77] White, Theodore D.; *An Outline of Shipbuilding Theoretical and Practical*; John Wiley & Son; New York; 1873; pp. 310.
[78] Lott, Arnold S., LCDR, USN; *A Long Line of Ships, Mare Island's Century of Naval Activity in California*, United States Naval Institute, Annapolis, MD, 1954, pp. 14.
[79] Lott, Arnold S., LCDR, USN; *A Long Line of Ships, Mare Island's Century of Naval Activity in California*, United States Naval Institute, Annapolis, MD, 1954, pp. 21-23.
[80] Lott, Arnold S., LCDR, USN; *A Long Line of Ships, Mare Island's Century of Naval Activity in California*, United States Naval Institute, Annapolis, MD, 1954, pp. 31.
[81] Lott, Arnold S., LCDR, USN; *A Long Line of Ships, Mare Island's Century of Naval Activity in California*, United States Naval Institute, Annapolis, MD, 1954, pp. 34.
[82] Stuart, Charles B.; *The Naval Dry Docks of the United States, Fourth Edition, Part Second, Floating Dry Docks*; D. Van Nostrand; New York, New York; 1870; pp. 8.
[83] http://members.xoom.com/ex_Yardbird/, Philadelphia Naval Shipyard Yard Bird website, 1998.
[84] Ibid.
[85] Stuart, Charles B.; *The Naval Dry Docks of the United States, Fourth Edition, Part Second, Floating Dry Docks*; D. Van Nostrand; New York, New York; 1870; pp.17.
[86] Stuart, Charles B.; *The Naval Dry Docks of the United States, Fourth Edition, Part Second, Floating Dry Docks*; D. Van Nostrand; New York, New York; 1870; pp. 20.
[87] White, Theodore D.; *An Outline of Shipbuilding Theoretical and Practical*; John Wiley & Son; New York; 1873; pp. 310.
[88] Stuart, Charles B.; *The Naval Dry Docks of the United States, Fourth Edition, Part Second, Floating Dry Docks*; D. Van Nostrand; New York, New York; 1870; pp. 11.
[89] Stuart, Charles B.; *The Naval Dry Docks of the United States, Fourth Edition, Part Second, Floating Dry Docks*; D. Van Nostrand; New York, New York; 1870; pp. 6.
[90] Donovan, Frank, *The Tall Frigates*, Dodd, Mead & Company, New York, NY, 1962, pp. 191-196.
[91] Ibid.

[92] Ibid.
[93] Rye, Scott; *Men and Ships of the Civil War*; Longmeadow Press, Stamford, CT, 1995; pp. 1-2.
[94] Ibid.
[95] Sweetman, Jack, *American Naval History*, Naval Institute Press, Annapolis, MD, 1991, pp. 65.
[96] www.netreach.net/~data/yardbird.htm; Philadelphia Naval Shipyard Yard Bird website, 1998.
[97] Tertius deKay, James; *MONITOR, The Story of the Legendary Civil War Ironclad and the Man Whose Invention Changed the Course of History*; Ballantine Books; New York, New York; 1997; pp. 46.
[98] Rye, Scott; *Men and Ships of the Civil War*; Longmeadow Press, Stamford, CT, 1995; pp. 4-6.
[99] Donovan, Frank, *The Tall Frigates*, Dodd, Mead & Company, New York, NY, 1962, pp. 200.
[100] Scharf, J. Thomas; *History of the Confederate States Navy*; Gramercy Books, New York, NY; pp.133.
[101] Sweetman, Jack, *American Naval History*, Naval Institute Press, Annapolis, MD, 1991, pp. 64.
[102] Marsh, C.C., CAPT, USN (Ret), *Official Records of the Union and Confederate Navies in the War of the Rebellion*; Washington, DC, 1921; pp. 784.
[103] Flanders, Alan B.; *The MERRIMAC: The Story of the Conversion of the USS MERRIMAC into the Confederate inronclad warship CSS VIRGINIA*; privately published; 1982; pp. 65.
[104] Rye, Scott; *Men and Ships of the Civil War*; Longmeadow Press, Stamford, CT, 1995; pp. 66.
[105] http://nnsy1.navy.mil; 2001.
[106] Sweetman, Jack, *American Naval History*, Naval Institute Press, Annapolis, MD, 1991, pp. 72.
[107] http://members.xoom.com/ex_Yardbird/, Philadelphia Naval Shipyard Yard Bird website, 1998.
[108] Ibid.
[109] Lott, Arnold S., LCDR, USN; *A Long Line of Ships, Mare Island's Century of Naval Activity in California*, United States Naval Institute, Annapolis, MD, 1954, pp. 93-94.
[110] http://members.xoom.com/ex_Yardbird/, Philadelphia Naval Shipyard Yard Bird website, 1998.
[111] *Building the Navy's Bases in World War II, History of the Bureau of yards and Docks and the Civil Engineer Corps 1940-*

[112] *1946 Volume 1*, United States Government Printing Office, Washington DC, 1947, pp. 169.

[112] Labaree, Benjamin W.; William M. Fowler, Jr.; Edward W. Sloan; John B. Hattendorf; Jeffery J. Safford; Andrew W. German; America and the Sea: A Maritime History; Mystic Seaport; 1998; pp. 387.

[113] Wilson, Theodore D., *An Outline of Shipbuilding Theoretical and Practical*, John Wiley & Son, New York, 1873, pp. 309-311.

[114] Lott, Arnold S., LCDR, USN; *A Long Line of Ships, Mare Island's Century of Naval Activity in California*, United States Naval Institute, Annapolis, MD, 1954, pp. 102.

[115] *Report of the Secretary of the Navy being part of The Message and Documents Communicated to the Two Houses of Congress at the Beginning of the First Session of the Fifty-First Congress*; Government Printing Office, Washington, D.C.; 1889; pp. 277.

[116] Lott, Arnold S., LCDR, USN; *A Long Line of Ships, Mare Island's Century of Naval Activity in California*, United States Naval Institute, Annapolis, MD, 1954, pp. 102.

[117] Lott, Arnold S., LCDR, USN; *A Long Line of Ships, Mare Island's Century of Naval Activity in California*, United States Naval Institute, Annapolis, MD, 1954, pp. 103.

[118] Lemmon, Sue and E. D. Wichels, Sidewheelers to Nuclear Power A Pictorial Essay Covering 125 Years at The Mare Island Naval Shipyard, 1977.

[119] Sprout, Harold and Margaret, *The Rise of American Naval Power 1776-1918*, Naval Institute Press, Annapolis, MD, 1966, pp. 215-216.

[120] Labaree, Benjamin W.; William M. Fowler, Jr.; Edward W. Sloan; John B. Hattendorf; Jeffery J. Safford; Andrew W. German; America and the Sea: A Maritime History; Mystic Seaport; 1998; pp. 389.

[121] Ibid.

[122] Gardiner, Robert; Conway's History of Ship, The Advent of Steam, the Merchant Ship before 1900; Chartweil Book's Inc.; 1993; pp. 23.

[123] Marshall W. Butt Library, Portsmouth Naval Shipyard Museum, Portsmouth, VA.

[124] Labaree, Benjamin W.; William M. Fowler, Jr.; Edward W. Sloan; John B. Hattendorf; Jeffery J. Safford; Andrew W. German; America and the Sea: A Maritime History; Mystic Seaport; 1998; pp. 442-444.

[125] Ibid.

[126] Naval Facilities Engineering Command, Design Manual Drydocking Facilities NAVFAC DM-29, Washington, DC, June 1969, pp. 29-11-74-75.

[127] *Report of the Secretary of the Navy being part of The Message and Documents Communicated to the Two Houses of Congress at the Beginning of the First Session of the Fifty-First Congress*; Government Printing Office, Washington, D.C.; 1889; pp. 176.

[128] Pearl Harbor Naval Shipyard, http://www.phnsy.navy.mil/phhistor.htm; Pearl Harbor Naval Shipyard Website, 1997; Pearl Harbor Shipyard Log; July 31, 1958

[129] Naval Historical Center, "Report of the Secretary of the Navy, 1898: Pacific Squadron", Naval Historical Center Website http://www.history.navy.mil/spanam/sn98-1.htm , Department of the Navy, Washington DC, February 1998.

[130] Portsmouth Naval Shipyard, "Cradle of American Shipbuilding", December 1978.

[131] Ibid.

[132] Lott, Arnold S., LCDR, USN; *A Long Line of Ships, Mare Island's Century of Naval Activity in California*, United States Naval Institute, Annapolis, MD, 1954, pp. 124-125.

[133] "Online Library of Selected Images, U.S. NAVY SHIPS", Department of the Navy, Naval Historical Center's website http://www.history.navy.mil, Washington D.C., January 2000.

[134] Churchill, Winston S.; *The Great Republic, A History of America*; Random House, New York, New York, 1999, pp. 240.

[135] Portsmouth Naval Shipyard, "Cradle of American Shipbuilding", December 1978.

[136] http://corregidor.org/chs_bogart/bogart1.htm

[137] Website of Rensselaer Polytechnic Institute (RPI), 110 8th St., Troy, NY 12180, http://www.rpi.edu/dept/NewsComm/sub/fame/inductees/mordecaiendicott.html , 2003.

[138] http://www.solomons-island.com/history.html

[139] Cook, Volney E., "General Discussion of Floating Dry docks", *Transactions*, Society of Naval Architects and Marine Engineers, New York, NY, November 1957, pp. 295.

[140] Bennet, LCDR F.M.; "The Voyage of the *DEWEY*", *The Proceedings of the United States Naval Institute Vol XXXII, No.4*, U.S. Naval Institute, Annapolis, Maryland, December 1906, pp. 1163-1212.

[141] Jarvis, Harry R., "Floating Docks", *Transactions of the North-East Coast Institution of Engineers and Shipbuilders, Vol XXIV, Twenty-Fourth Session*, 1907-1908, New Castle-Upon Tyne and London, Andrew Reid & Company, Limited, Printers and Publishers, 1908, pp. 211.

[142] *Building the Navy's Bases in World War II, History of the Bureau of yards and Docks and the Civil Engineer Corps 1940-1946 Volume I*, United States Government Printing Office, Washington DC, 1947, pp. 169.

[143] Bureau of Construction and Repair, Bulletin No. 19, U.S. Navy Department, Washington, D.C., March 30, 1909, pp. 9.

[144] Bureau of Construction and Repair, Bulletin No. 19, U.S. Navy Department, Washington, D.C., March 30, 1909, pp. 9.

[145] Pearl Harbor Shipyard Log; July 31, 1958

[146] Gilbert, Martin; *Churchill, A Life*; Henry Holt and Company; New York, NY; 1991; pp. 209.

[147] Gilbert, Martin; *Churchill, A Life*; Henry Holt and Company; New York, NY; 1991; pp. 202.

[148] Lott, Arnold S., LCDR, USN; *A Long Line of Ships, Mare Island's Century of Naval Activity in California*, United States Naval Institute, Annapolis, MD, 1954, pp. 146-147.

[149] Naval Facilities Engineering Command, Design Manual Drydocking Facilities NAVFAC DM-29, Washington, DC, June 1969, pp. 29-11-92-93.

[150] Sweetman, Jack, *American Naval History*, Naval Institute Press, Annapolis, MD, 1991, pp. 120-121.

[151] Pearl Harbor Shipyard Log; July 31, 1958

[152] Pearl Harbor Shipyard Log; July 31, 1958

[153] Shaw, James L.; Ships of the Panama Canal; Naval Institute Press; Annapolis, Maryland; 1985; pp. 27.

[154] Bureau of Construction and Repair, Bulletin No. 57, U.S. Navy Department, Washington D.C., July 1, 1914.

[155] Reynolds, Francis J.; *The United States Navy, From the Revolution to Date*; P.F. Collier & Son; New York; 1916; pp. 141-144.

[156] Sweetman, Jack, *American Naval History*, Naval Institute Press, Annapolis, MD, 1991, pp. 138.

[157] http://members.xoom.com/ex_Yardbird/, Philadelphia Naval Shipyard Yard Bird website, 1998.

[158] Sweetman, Jack, *American Naval History*, Naval Institute Press, Annapolis, MD, 1991, pp. 138.

[159] Labaree, Benjamin W.; William M. Fowler, Jr.; Edward W. Sloan; John B. Hattendorf; Jeffery J. Safford; Andrew W.

German; America and the Sea: A Maritime History; Mystic Seaport; 1998; pp. 500.

[160] Marshall W. Butt Library, Portsmouth Naval Shipyard Museum, Portsmouth, VA.

[161] Pearl Harbor Shipyard Log; July 31, 1958

[162] Naval Facilities Engineering Command, Design Manual Drydocking Facilities NAVFAC DM-29, Washington, DC, June 1969, pp. 29-11-146-147.

[163] http://members.xoom.com/ex_Yardbird/, Philadelphia Naval Shipyard Yard Bird website, 1998.

[164] United States Navy Regulations, United States Government Printing Office, 1920.

[165] Potter, E.B.; *Sea Power, Second Edition*; United States Naval Institute; Annapolis, Maryland, 1981; pp. 233.

[166] Labaree, Benjamin W.; William M. Fowler, Jr.; Edward W. Sloan; John B. Hattendorf; Jeffery J. Safford; Andrew W. German; America and the Sea: A Maritime History; Mystic Seaport; 1998; pp. 508-509.

[167] Ibid..

[168] Naval Facilities Engineering Command, Design Manual Drydocking Facilities NAVFAC DM-29, Washington, DC, June 1969, pp. 29-11-122-123.

[169] Gayhart, LCDR E. L., (CC) USN, "An Analysis of a Failure of Keel Blocks in a Dry dock", *TRANSACTIONS Vol XXXIII*, The Society of Naval Architects and Marine Engineers, New York, New York, November 1925, pp. 161.

[170] *Building the Navy's Bases in World War II, History of the Bureau of yards and Docks and the Civil Engineer Corps 1940-1946 Volume I*, United States Government Printing Office, Washington DC, 1947, pp. 169.

[171] Sweetman, Jack; *American Naval History, An Illustrated History of the U.S. Navy and Marine Corps, 1775-Present*; Naval Institute Press, Annapolis, MD; pp. 151-157.

[172] Department of the Navy, Naval Historical Center, http://www.history.navy.mil/photos/sh-usn/usnsh-h/cv8.htm

[173] Department of the Navy, Chief of Naval Information;

[174] Department of the Navy, Chief of Naval Information; http://www.chinfo.navy.mil/navpalib/ships/carriers/histories/cv05-yorktown/cv05-yorktown.html

[175] Potter, E.B.; *Sea Power, A Naval History, Second Edition*, United States Naval Institute, Annapolis, Maryland; pp. 242.

[176] http://www.microworks.net/pacific/biographies/ben_moreell htm

[177] *Building the Navy's Bases in World War II, History of the Bureau of yards and Docks and the Civil Engineer Corps 1940-1946 Volume I*, United States Government Printing Office, Washington DC, 1947, pp. 170.

[178] *Building the Navy's Bases in World War II, History of the Bureau of yards and Docks and the Civil Engineer Corps 1940-1946 Volume I*, United States Government Printing Office, Washington DC, 1947, pp. 178.

[179] *Building the Navy's Bases in World War II, History of the Bureau of yards and Docks and the Civil Engineer Corps 1940-1946 Volume II*, United States Government Printing Office, Washington DC, 1947, pp. 124.

[146] Gilbert, Martin; *Churchill, A Life*; Henry Holt and Company; New York, NY; 1991; pp. 209.

[147] Gilbert, Martin; *Churchill, A Life*; Henry Holt and Company; New York, NY; 1991; pp. 202.

[148] Lott, Arnold S., LCDR, USN; *A Long Line of Ships, Mare Island's Century of Naval Activity in California*, United States Naval Institute, Annapolis, MD, 1954, pp. 146-147.

[149] Naval Facilities Engineering Command, Design Manual Drydocking Facilities NAVFAC DM-29, Washington, DC, June 1969, pp. 29-11-92-93.

[150] Sweetman, Jack, *American Naval History*, Naval Institute Press, Annapolis, MD, 1991, pp. 120-121.

[151] Pearl Harbor Shipyard Log; July 31, 1958

[152] Pearl Harbor Shipyard Log; July 31, 1958

[153] Shaw, James L.; Ships of the Panama Canal; Naval Institute Press; Annapolis, Maryland; 1985; pp. 27.

[154] Bureau of Construction and Repair, Bulletin No. 57, U.S. Navy Department, Washington D.C., July 1, 1914.

[155] Reynolds, Francis J.; *The United States Navy, From the Revolution to Date*; P.F. Collier & Son; New York; 1916; pp. 141-144.

[156] Sweetman, Jack, *American Naval History*, Naval Institute Press, Annapolis, MD, 1991, pp. 138.

[157] http://members.xoom.com/ex_Yardbird/, Philadelphia Naval Shipyard Yard Bird website, 1998.

[158] Sweetman, Jack, *American Naval History*, Naval Institute Press, Annapolis, MD, 1991, pp. 138.

[159] Labaree, Benjamin W.; William M. Fowler, Jr.; Edward W. Sloan; John B. Hattendorf; Jeffery J. Safford; Andrew W. German; America and the Sea: A Maritime History; Mystic Seaport; 1998; pp. 500.

[160] Marshall W. Butt Library, Portsmouth Naval Shipyard Museum, Portsmouth, VA.

[161] Pearl Harbor Shipyard Log; July 31, 1958

[162] Naval Facilities Engineering Command, Design Manual Drydocking Facilities NAVFAC DM-29, Washington, DC, June 1969, pp. 29-11-146-147.

[163] http://members.xoom.com/ex_Yardbird/, Philadelphia Naval Shipyard Yard Bird website, 1998.

[164] United States Navy Regulations, United States Government Printing Office, 1920.

[165] Potter, E.B.; *Sea Power, Second Edition*; United States Naval Institute; Annapolis, Maryland, 1981; pp. 233.

[166] Labaree, Benjamin W.; William M. Fowler, Jr.; Edward W. Sloan; John B. Hattendorf; Jeffery J. Safford; Andrew W. German; America and the Sea: A Maritime History; Mystic Seaport; 1998; pp. 508-509.

[167] Ibid..

[168] Naval Facilities Engineering Command, Design Manual Drydocking Facilities NAVFAC DM-29, Washington, DC, June 1969, pp. 29-11-122-123.

[169] Gayhart, LCDR E. L., (CC) USN, "An Analysis of a Failure of Keel Blocks in a Dry dock", *TRANSACTIONS Vol XXXIII*, The Society of Naval Architects and Marine Engineers, New York, New York, November 1925, pp. 161.

[170] *Building the Navy's Bases in World War II, History of the Bureau of yards and Docks and the Civil Engineer Corps 1940-1946 Volume I*, United States Government Printing Office, Washington DC, 1947, pp. 169.

[171] Sweetman, Jack; *American Naval History, An Illustrated History of the U.S. Navy and Marine Corps, 1775-Present*; Naval Institute Press, Annapolis, MD; pp. 151-157.

[172] Department of the Navy, Naval Historical Center, http://www.history.navy.mil/photos/sh-usn/usnsh-h/cv8.htm

[173] Department of the Navy, Chief of Naval Information;

[174] Department of the Navy, Chief of Naval Information; http://www.chinfo.navy.mil/navpalib/ships/carriers/histories/cv05-yorktown/cv05-yorktown.html

[175] Potter, E.B.; *Sea Power, A Naval History, Second Edition*, United States Naval Institute, Annapolis, Maryland; pp. 242.

[176] http://www.microworks.net/pacific/biographies/ben_moreell.htm

[177] *Building the Navy's Bases in World War II, History of the Bureau of yards and Docks and the Civil Engineer Corps*

[177] *1940-1946 Volume I*, United States Government Printing Office, Washington DC, 1947, pp. 170.

[178] *Building the Navy's Bases in World War II, History of the Bureau of yards and Docks and the Civil Engineer Corps 1940-1946 Volume I*, United States Government Printing Office, Washington DC, 1947, pp. 178.

[179] *Building the Navy's Bases in World War II, History of the Bureau of yards and Docks and the Civil Engineer Corps 1940-1946 Volume II*, United States Government Printing Office, Washington DC, 1947, pp. 124.

[180] *Building the Navy's Bases in World War II, History of the Bureau of yards and Docks and the Civil Engineer Corps 1940-1946 Volume I*, United States Government Printing Office, Washington DC, 1947, pp. 173.

[181] National Academy Press, Memorial Tributes (1991), William Henry Mueser, http://books.nap.edu/books/0309043492/html/259.html

[182] *Building the Navy's Bases in World War II, History of the Bureau of yards and Docks and the Civil Engineer Corps 1940-1946 Volume I*, United States Government Printing Office, Washington DC, 1947, pp. 175.

[183] Sweetman, Jack; *American Naval History, An Illustrated History of the U.S. Navy and Marine Corps, 1775-Present*; Naval Institute Press, Annapolis, MD; pp. 157-158.

[184] *Building the Navy's Bases in World War II, History of the Bureau of yards and Docks and the Civil Engineer Corps 1940-1946 Volume I*, United States Government Printing Office, Washington DC, 1947, pp. 172.

[185] Ibid.

[186] *Building the Navy's Bases in World War II, History of the Bureau of yards and Docks and the Civil Engineer Corps 1940-1946 Volume I*, United States Government Printing Office, Washington DC, 1947, pp. 182.

[187] http://corregidor.org/chs_munson/wint.htm

[188] Moore, George F., Major General, U.S. Army (Formerly Commanding the Philippine Coast Artillery Command and the Harbor Defenses of Manila and Subic Bays), "THE MOORE REPORT", http://corregidor.org/chs_moorerpt/moore2.htm#G1

[189] Wallin, Vice Admiral Homer N. USN (Retired); *Pearl Harbor: Why, How, Fleet Salvage and Final Appraisal*; United States Government Printing Office, Naval History Division; Washington D.C.; 1968; pp. 203.

[190] Cohen, Stan, *East Wind Rain, A Pictorial History of the Pearl harbor Attack*, Pictorial Histories Publishing Company, Missoula, Montana, 1981.

[191] Wallin, Vice Admiral Homer N. USN (Retired); *Pearl Harbor: Why, How, Fleet Salvage and Final Appraisal*; United States Government Printing Office, Naval History Division; Washington D.C.; 1968; pp. 204-206.

[192] Ibid.

[193] Naval Historical Center, "Ships Present at Pearl Harbor, 0800 7 December 1941", Naval Historical Center Website http://www.history.navy.mil/faqs/faq66-1.htm , Department of the Navy, Washington DC, November 1997.

[194] *Building the Navy's Bases in World War II, History of the Bureau of yards and Docks and the Civil Engineer Corps 1940-1946 Volume II*, United States Government Printing Office, Washington DC, 1947, pp. 124.

[195] Dry Dock Facility Characteristics, Military Handbook 1029/3, Naval Facilities Engineering Command Alexandria, VA, 1988, pp 83.

[196] http://fourthmarinesband.com/shanghai.htm

[197] http://justgosubic.lakbay.net/aboutus.asp

[198] http://www.subicbaymarines.com/SBM1/history.htm

[199] http://www.ibiblio.org/hyperwar/USN/ships/YFD/YFD-1_Dewey.html

[200] SRF History, http://www.geocities.com/TheTropics/9586/srf.html

[201] http://users3.ev1.net/~de238/stewart/history006.htm

[202] Yarnall, Paul R., http://www.navsource.org/Archives/CV/cv5.htm, NavSource Naval History. 1998.

[203] *Building the Navy's Bases in World War II, History of the Bureau of yards and Docks and the Civil Engineer Corps 1940-1946 Volume II*, United States Government Printing Office, Washington DC, 1947, pp. 126.

[204] Dry Dock Facility Characteristics, Military Handbook 1029/3, Naval Facilities Engineering Command Alexandria, VA, 1988.

[205] http://www.microworks.net/pacific/biographies/ben_moreell.htm

[206] Cook, Volney E., "General Discussion of Floating Dry docks", *Transactions*, The Society of Naval Architects and Marine Engineers, November 1957, pp. 290.

[207] *Drydocking Facilities, Vol. 3 Data Book*; "Dry dock Characteristic Summary Department of the Navy Bureau of Yards and Docks", Washington D.C.; 1955.

[208] Jackson, CAPT Harry A., USN (ret), Discussion of Mr. Volney E. Cook's "General Discussion of Floating Dry docks", *Transactions*, The Society of Naval Architects and Marine Engineers, November 1957, pp. 300.
[209] Cook, Volney E., "General Discussion of Floating Dry docks", *Transactions*, The Society of Naval Architects and Marine Engineers, November 1957, pp. 292.
[210] "Warship International Vol. XVI, No. 1, 1979,"; The International Naval Research Organization, Inc.; Toledo, Ohio; 1979; pp. 1.
[211] Angas, CAPT W. Mack, CEC, USN; "Seagoing Navy Yard Follows the Fleet"; *Popular Science*, November 1945, pp. 121-122.
[212] Smith, RADM W. H., (CEC) USN (Ret), Discussion of Mr. Volney E. Cook's "General Discussion of Floating Dry docks", *Transactions*, The Society of Naval Architects and Marine Engineers, November 1957, pp. 305-306.
[213] "The Years of Combat, 1965-1968", Department of the Navy, Naval Historical Center, Washington DC, January 2000.
[214] Polmar, Norman; *Ships and Aircraft of the U.S. Fleet*; Naval Institute Press, Annapolis, MD; 1997.
[215] *Drydocking Facilities, Vol 3 Data Book Dry dock Characteristic Summary*; Department of the Navy Bureau of Yards and Docks, Washington D.C.; 1955.
[216] Ibid..
[217] *Drydocking Facilities, Vol 3 Data Book*; "Dry dock Characteristic Summary Department of the Navy Bureau of Yards and Docks, Washington D.C.; 1955; pp. 286.
[218] SYNCROLIFT©, Shiplifts & Transfer Systems, Miami, Florida.
[219] SYNCROLIFT©, Shiplifts & Transfer Systems, Miami, Florida.
[220] Stokoe, Geoff A.; Syncrolift, Inc. Letter, April 15, 1997.
[221] ARGONAUTICS Marine Engineering, Sausalito, CA, 1996.
[222] Polmar, Norman; *Ships and Aircraft of the U.S. Fleet*; Naval Institute Press, Annapolis, MD; 1997, pp. Appendix A.
[223] *Marine Log*, Vol. 102, No. 6, June 1997, pp. 31-35.
[224] Ibid.
[225] Sahagun, Louis; Really Big Doings at the Ports; Los Angeles Times, Thursday March 28, 2002, page 1.
[226] *Maritime Reporter and Engineering News*, Vol. 59 No. 7, New York, NY, July 1997, pp. 48.
[227] Thorpe, Alan, International Editor, "Where Do You Dry dock a Postpanamax", *Marine Log*, December 1999, pp. 38.

[228] Helprin, Mark; "The Fire Next Time"; *Wall Street Journal*; April 24, 2001.
[229] Congress of the United States, Congressional Budget Office Study, *"Transforming the Navy's Surface Combatant Force"*, March 2003, pp. xi.

Figures

Figure 1 - Drawing of the first marine railway in the United States at the Washington Navy Yard designed in 1822 by Commodore John Rodgers. (*Government Printing Office*) 13

Figure 2 - "Sketch of the Position of the Works of the Dry dock" as it was on November 1, 1829 at the Gosport Navy Yard, Portsmouth, Virginia. (National Archives) 15

Figure 3 - Close-up of excavation status of the first dry dock constructed in United States. This drawing depicted the status of excavation as of November 1, 1829. (National Archives) 16

Figure 4 - Close-up of the explanation section of November 27, 1829 excavation and Gosport Navy Yard "Sketch of the Position of the Works of the Dry dock". The engineer was Loammi Baldwin whose signature appears on this sketch. (National Archives) 17

Figure 5 - Sketch of the state of the work on the first dry dock in the United States at the Gosport Navy Yard near Norfolk, Virginia as it was on May 10, 1832. L. Baldwin was the engineer. (National Archives) ... 18

Figure 6 - Sketch of the status of work on the near completed dry dock with the gates in place at the Gosport Navy Yard near Norfolk, Virginia as it was on November 2, 1832. (National Archives) 19

Figure 7 - Gate at the entrance to the Gosport Dry dock as it was on November 2, 1832. (National Archives). .. 19

Figure 8 - *USS DELAWARE* entering the Gosport Dry dock at Norfolk June 17, 1833. This was the first drydocking in the United States. (Naval Historical Center) 21

Figure 9 – *"USS DELAWARE* in the Gosport Dry dock at Norfolk 17 June 1833". (Naval Historical Center) 23

Figure 10 - Title of the first Plan for a Dry Dock at New York. (National Archives).. 26

Figure 11 - *USS PENNSYLVANIA* depicted in new dry dock at New York Navy Yard. (Naval Historical Center)..... 26

Figure 12 - Dedication page of Charles B. Stuart's 1852 book to President Fillmore. (Naval Historical Center)....... 27

Figure 13 - Drawing of the status of work of the United States Dry dock in New York as of October 1, 1848 (National Archives)... 28

Figure 14 - This is a close-up view of the New York Dry dock and surrounding area on October 1, 1848 showing the site of the building for the engines and pumps. (National Archives) 29

Figure 15 - Drawing of the engine house adjacent to the New York dry dock. (Naval Historical Center) 30

Figure 16 - Graving dock at New York Navy Yard plan view and the pump well, receiving, and discharge culverts. (Naval Historical Center)........................... 31

Figure 17 - Side elevation of Engine and Pumps and Longitudinal Section of Well. (Naval Historical Center).. 31

Figure 18 - Culvert Gate mechanism for the New York Dry Dock. (Naval Historical Center)........................ 32

Figure 19 - This is an 1849 isometric drawing of the graving dock that was to become Dry Dock Nr. 1 at what became the Brooklyn Navy Yard, New York. (National Archives).. 33

Figure 20 - Drawing of the completed dry dock at New York showing cross sections (one with *USS PENNSYLVANIA* in dock) and side view. (Naval Historical Center).. 34

Figure 21 - Construction drawing of the first dry dock on the West Coast of the United States. Drawing dated May 19, 1851. (National Archives)................ 38

Figure 22 - Top view looking down on top of wing wall and half of dock floor on one section of the first sectional floating dry dock at Mare Island Navy

Yard. (National Archives) 38

Figure 23 - Close-up of the end view looking longitudinally at one of the Mare Island floating dry dock wingwall and ballast tank sections. (National Archives) 40

Figure 24 - Close-up of the end view looking longitudinally at one of the Mare Island floating dry dock floor sections. (National Archives) 41

Figure 25 - *USS PORTSMOUTH*. One of the first ships drydocked in the floating dry dock at the Mare Island Navy Yard. (National Archives) 44

Figure 26 - Drawing of Philadelphia Sectional Dry Dock completed June 5th 1851. (Naval Historical Center).. 46

Figure 27 - Sketch of a sectional dry dock and a steamer being transferred to a land level facility. (Naval Historical Center) 48

Figure 28 - Sketch of proposed arrangement of pumping engines for the Norfolk Navy Yard. Drawn in New York on April 24, 1855. (National Archives) ... 49

Figure 29 - Estimate of the cost of construction of a second dry dock at the Gosport Yard in 1857. (National Archives) 50

Figure 30 - Proposed 2nd dry dock at Norfolk cost estimate percentages in 1857. 52

Figure 31 - *EX-USS MERRIMACK* [*CSS VIRGINIA*] in dry dock at the Norfolk Navy Yard under the Confederate Navy control May 1861. (Naval Historical Center)... 57

Figure 32 - Drawing of the first dry dock at Hunters' Point near San Francisco 1868. (National Archives) 61

Figure 33 - Close up of the approved site for the location of the second dry dock at Norfolk Navy Yard April 26, 1887. (National Archives) 67

Figure 34 - Wider view of the site drawing and approval statement for the location of the proposed Norfolk Navy Yard. A new timber dry dock was selected by a Naval board of officers on April 26, 1887 and approved by the Chief of Bureau of Yards and Docks on April 27m 1887. (National Archives) 67

Figure 35 - Reference block on the drawing showing the site for the 2nd dry dock at Norfolk Navy yard approved on April 27, 1887. (National Archives) 68

Figure 36 - Rest of the Norfolk Navy Yard as is was on April 27, 1887. (National Archives) 69

Figure 37 - *USS AILEEN* in dry dock at the New York Navy Yard, Brooklyn, New York, while being converted for naval service, May 17, 1898. (Naval Historical Center Photograph Photo #: NH 57751*)* 74

Figure 38 - Notes from the August 1, 1899 Schedule of Quantities drawing for the construction of Dry Dock Nr. 2 at the League Island (Philadelphia) Navy Yard. (National Archives) 75

Figure 39 - Schedule of Quantities for the Dry dock Proper and Culvert sections of the August 1, 1899 drawing for the construction of Dry Dock Nr. 2 at the League Island (Philadelphia) Navy Yard. (National Archives) 76

Figure 40 - Schedule of Quantities for the Caisson section of the August 1, 1899 drawing for the construction of Dry Dock Nr. 2 at the League Island (Philadelphia) Navy Yard. (National Archives) 76

Figure 41 - Schedule of Quantities for the Power and Boiler House section of the August 1, 1899 drawing for the construction of Dry Dock Nr. 2 at the League Island Philadelphia) Navy Yard. (National Archives) 77

Figure 42 - Title Block for the Details of the Blocks and Fittings for Dry Dock Nr. 2 at the League Island (Philadelphia) Navy Yard. (National Archives) 77

Figure 43 - End and plan view of the side (bilge) block slides for Dry Dock Nr. 2 at the League Island (Philadelphia) Navy Yard. (National Archives) 78

Figure 44 - Close-up of outboard end of a typical side (bilge) block slide for Dry Dock Nr. 2 at the League Island (Philadelphia) Navy Yard. (National Archives) 80

Figure 45 - Close-up of inboard end of a typical side (bilge) block slide pulley for Dry Dock Nr. 2 at the League

Island (Philadelphia) Navy Yard. (National Archives) 81

Figure 46 - Bureau of Yards and Docks drawing legend for the Stone and Concrete Dry dock at the League Island (Philadelphia), PA Navy Yard May 1900. (National Archives) 82

Figure 47 - Bureau of Yards and Docks cross-section drawing for the Stone and Concrete Dry dock at the League Island (Philadelphia), PA Navy Yard May 1900. (National Archives) 82

Figure 48 - The Battleship *USS IOWA* entering Dry Dock Nr. 1 in 1900 at Puget Sound Navy Yard. (U.S. Navy Photo). 83

Figure 49 - *USS ILLINOIS (BB 7)* in floating dry dock during the dock's load and operational test January 6, 1902. (Naval Historical Center). 86

Figure 50 - *USS Cleveland* (Cruiser # 19) In the *DEWEY* dry dock, Olongapo Naval Station, Philippine Islands, January 14, 1908. (Naval Historical Center). 88

Figure 51 - Stern view of USS *Cleveland* (Cruiser # 19) in the *DEWEY* dry dock, Olongapo Naval Station, Philippine Islands, January 14, 1908. (Naval Historical Center). 88

Figure 52 - Plan of dry docks at Hunters Point (San Francisco Dry Dock Company) near San Francisco, California 1907. (National Archives). 90

Figure 53 - Title section of drawing of dry docks at Hunters Point (San Francisco Dry Dock Company) near San Francisco, California 1907. (National Archives). 91

Figure 54 - Puget Sound Navy Yard Dry Dock 2 under construction. Construction began in 1909 and completed in 1912. (U.S. Navy photo) 93

Figure 55 - Title section of Bureau of Yards and Docks construction drawing of the Norfolk Navy Yard Sluice Gate chamber for Dry Dock Nr. 4 approved September 11, 1916 (National Archives). 96

Figure 56 - Bureau of Yards and Docks construction drawing of the Norfolk Navy Yard Dry Dock Nr. 4 Sluice Gate chamber approved September 11, 1916 (National Archives) 97

Figure 57 - First drydocking in Dry Dock Nr. 4 Norfolk Navy Yard on May 5, 1919. Ship is the *USS WISCONSIN*. The *USS NEVADA* is in Dry Dock Nr. 3 to the left in this photo. (National Archives) 99

Figure 58 - Close-up of *USS WISCONSIN* in Dry Dock Nr. 4 Norfolk Naval Shipyard May 5, 1919. (National Archives) 100

Figure 59 - Opening ceremony of Dry Dock Nr. 1 at Pearl Harbor Navy Yard. (U.S. Navy Photo) 100

Figure 60 - Status of construction drawing in 1919 of Dry Dock Nr. 3 at the Philadelphia Navy Yard. Dates indicate when sections were completed. (National Archives) 102

Figure 61 - *USS DELAWARE (BB 28)* on January 30, 1924 during scrapping at the South Boston Annex, Boston Navy Yard. (Naval Historical Center) 103

Figure 62 - *USS DELAWARE* in dry dock at South Boston, January 30, 1924. (National Archives) 104

Figure 63 - Part of drawing of Dry Dock Nr. 3 (caisson end) Philadelphia Navy Yard (U.S. Navy, Bureau of Yards and Docks U.S. Navy) 105

Figure 64 - Philadelphia Naval Shipyard Dry Dock Nr. 3 drawing showing electric dewatering pump. (National Archives). 107

Figure 65 - *USS ARKANSAS* in Dry Dock Nr.3 at Philadelphia Naval Shipyard 15 October 1926. (National Archives) 108

Figure 66 - Pre-World War II photo of Norfolk Naval Shipyard Dry Dock Nr. 4 with one of first aircraft carriers in the dock. (National Archives) 109

Figure 67 - *USS RANGER (CV 4)*, first aircraft carrier built from the keel up, launched at Newport News Shipbuilding and Dry Dock Company February 25, 1933. (U.S. Navy Photo). 110

Figure 68 - *USS YORKTOWN (CV 5)* at the Newport News

Shipbuilding and Dry Dock Company, Newport News, Virginia, in June 1937. *USS ENTERPRISE (CV 6)* is being fitted out in dry dock also seen in upper left of this figure. (U. S. Navy Photo) 111

Figure 69 - Puget Sound Navy Yard Dry Dock Nr. 4 opening in 1940. (U. S. Navy Photo).. 114

Figure 70 - Forward magazine of *USS SHAW* exploding while in the floating dry dock at Pearl Harbor Navy Yard December 7, 1941. (U.S. Navy Photo) 119

Figure 71 - December 7, 1941 at the Pearl Harbor Navy Yard, two destroyers, the *USS CASSIN (DD372)* and the *USS DOWNES (DD375)* were in Dry Dock Nr. 1 with the battleship *USS PENNSYLVANIA (BB38)*.................. 121

Figure 72 - *USS CASSIN* under salvage in the same drydock attacked at Pearl Harbor Navy Yard January 23, 1942. *(*Naval Historical Center*)* 122

Figure 73 - Pearl Harbor Naval Shipyard with locations of the four graving dry docks. 123

Figure 74 - *USS YORKTOWN (CV-5)* In dry dock at Pearl Harbor, repairing her damage from the Battle of Coral Sea, Just prior to sailing for Midway. She was sunk less than a week later during the Battle of Midway June 1942. 125

Figure 75 - Map of Philadelphia Navy Yard (left) and Norfolk Navy Yard (right). (U.S. Navy)............................... 127

Figure 76 - Long Beach (Terminal Island) Navy Yard Dry Dock Nr. 1 opened 1942. Insert is *USS MISSOURI (BB63)* in this graving dock in August 1984. (official U.S. Navy Photo). 128

Figure 77 - Hunters Point Navy Yard. (U.S. Navy Photo). 128

Figure 78 - New York Navy yard with all graving docks completed on March 9, 1944. (U.S. Navy Photo) 129

Figure 79 - *USS ANTELOPE (IX-109)* In the floating dry dock *ABSD-1* at Espiritu Santo, New Hebrides, January 8, 1945. Also in the dry dock, astern of *Antelope* is *USS LST-120*. *YF-326* is the nearest of the yardcraft on the right, moored to *ABSD-1*. *(U.S. Navy Photos)* 136

Figure 80 - *USS ANTELOPE (IX-109)* Entering the floating dry dock *ABSD-1* at Espiritu Santo, New Hebrides, January 5, 1945. (U.S. Navy Photo)........................ 137

Figure 81 - *USS RESOLUTE* at the Naval Operating Base (NOB) Norfolk, Virginia 1996 (U.S. Navy Photo)............... 138

Figure 82 - Cross section drawing of an AFDB floating dry dock with wing wall crane. (U.S. Navy drawing)............. 139

Figure 83 - *USS SPRUANCE (DD-963)* In the floating dry dock at the Ingalls shipyard, Pascagoula, Mississippi, while being prepared for builders' trials, circa January 1975. (U.S. Navy Photo) 141

Figure 84 - Plot of the number of graving dry docks completed in a particular year.................................. 146

Figure 85 - Length of graving dry dock versus year completed. 146

Figure 86 - *USS MISSOURI (BB 63)* upon entering Dry Dock Nr. 1, Long Beach Naval Shipyard August 1984. (U.S. Navy photo).. 147

Figure 87 - Marine railway as it was in 1955 at the Washington D.C. Naval gun Factory. Site of the first marine railway in United States. (U.S Navy) 150

Figure 88 - *USS ELLIOTT (DD 967)* Being Towed off SYNCROLIFT© at Todd Pacific Shipyard Los Angeles in 1984. (Courtesy SYNCROLIFT)........... 151

Figure 89 - Largest SYNCROLIFT© in the world in Los Angeles 1984. Was moved to Malaysia in 1997. (Courtesy SYNCROLIFT, Inc.).............................. 154

Figure 90 - *SUPER SERVANT 3* with (3) MSO's and (1) MCM leaving Little Creek Naval Amphibious Base August 29, 1990 underway to Arabian Gulf. (Photo by Richard D. Hepburn) 156

Figure 91 - *USS OSPREY (MHC 51)* on floodable barge being transported in Chesapeake Bay to Aberdeen Proving Grounds for shock testing. (Photo courtesy Jim Sandison)................................. 157

Figure 92 - *USS OSPREY (MHC 51)* on a floodable barge, in a graving dock at Norfolk Naval Shipyard. (courtesy of Jim Sandison)... 158

Figure 93 - Change in number of U.S. Navy graving docks since 1968.. 162

Figure 94 - Arrival of *USS COLE (DDG 67)* on heavy lift ship *M/V BLUE MARLIN* at Pascogoula, Mississippi, December 13, 2000. (U.S. Navy Photo) 164

Figure 95 - The Ex Hunters Point Naval Shipyard Dry Dock #4 in 1999 with ship scrapping in progress. (U.S. Navy Photo)... 164

Figure 96 - Ex Long Beach Naval Shipyard and Naval Station on October 7, 2002. Two of three dry docks have been filled in at the shipyard as the entire complex was turned into a container port. (Photo by Debra A. Hepburn).. 170

Tables

Table 1 - 1857 estimated cost to build a second
graving dry dock at Norfolk Navy Yard.................. 51

Table 2 - Graving docks completed during
World War II (1942 through 1944)........................ 130

Table 3 - Classes and numbers of U.S. Navy Floating
dry docks as of February 1, 1955 (U.S. Navy)......... 134

Table 4 - All U.S. Navy owned graving dry docks,
locations, dry dock number, date completed,
and the length of the dock that existed
February 1, 1955 143

Table 5 - Nine additional graving dry docks after
World War II... 145

Table 6 - Estimates of the U.S. Navy owned graving
docks still in operation as of June 1999.................. 161

Table 7 - Estimates of the U.S. Navy owned floating dry
docks still in operation as of June 1999.................. 162

Table 8 - Reduction iN numbers of U.S. Naval warships
from 1955 to 2003... 163

Index

ABSD, 134, 135, 136, 137
ADROIT, 155
AFDB, 134, 138, 139
AFDM, 137,
AILEEN, 73, 74
ALABAMA, 91
ANTELOPE, 136, 137
ARD, 133, 134,
ARIZONA, 96
ARKANSAS, 106, 108
ARLEIGH BURKE, 136
ATLANTA, 65, 66
AVENGER, 155
Babcock & Wilcox, 91
Balboa, Canal Zone, 95
Baldwin, Loammi, 4, 13, 14, 16, 18, 20, 23, 25, 24, 25, 54
BARBOUR COUNTY, 152, 153
Base Realignment and Closure, 169
Bataan, 118, 122
Bath Iron Works, 47, 140, 169
BLUE MARLIN, 136, 163
BOSTON, 11, 66, 130, 143, 144, 145
Boston Navy Yard, 116
Bruff, J. G., 20, 21, 22
BRUTUS, 87
Bureau of Ships, 115
Bureau of Yards and Docks, 34, 43, 67, 77, 82, 85, 96, 97, 105, 112, 113, 115, 116, 127, 130, 133, 135
CAESER, 87
caisson, 2, 19, 32, 75, 76, 89, 99, 100, 101, 104, 105, 113, 123
CALIFORNIA, 91
CASSIN, 120, 121
Cavite Naval Yard, 85
Chandler, William E., 65
Charleston, 124, 125, 139
Charleston Navy Yard, 92, 116
Charlestown Navy Yard, 8, 13, 15, 23
CHESAPEAKE, 6, 7
Chief of the Bureau of Yards and Docks, 43, 67, 77, 85, 112, 113, 127

I-1

Churchill, Winston, 83, 92
CLEVELAND, 87, 88
COLE, 155, 163, 164
COLORADO, 86, 104
CONNECTICUT, 91
CONSTELLATION, 6
CONSTITUTION, 6, 23, 36, 60
Cristobal Canal Zone, 104
CUMBERLAND, 55, 57
Daniels, Joseph Francis, 43, 112
DELAWARE, 11, 20, 21, 22, 23, 23, 53, 55, 96, 103, 104
DESTINY, 168
DEWEY, 86, 87, 88, 117, 118, 122, 123, 124
DOLPHIN, 65
Dry Dock Nr. 1 at New York Navy Yard, 32
Dry Dock Nr. 4 Norfolk Navy Yard, 99
EAGLE, 168
ELLIOTT, 150, 151, 152, 154
Endicott, Mordecai T., 85
ENTERPRISE, 8, 110, 111, 145
ESSEX, 112
Farragut, David, 42
floating dry dock at Pearl Harbor Navy Yard, 119
floodable barge, 149, 156, 157, 158, 161
FLORIDA, 96
FRANKLIN, 36
GENERAL GREEN, 11
GLACIER, 87
Gosport Navy Yard, 15, 17, 18, 36
Great White Fleet, 85, 91
Haswell, Charles H., 34
Hawaiian God Kaahupahau, 93
heavy lift ship, 136, 139, 149, 155,
HELENA, 123
HOEL, 147
HORNET, 110, 111
Humphrey's, Joshua, 6, 7, 25
Hunt, William H., 65
Hunters Point Navy Yard, 60, 61, 90, 91, 128, 145, 165,
ILLINOIS, 86
IMPERVIOUS, 155
INDEPENDENCE, 62
Ingalls (NGSS) Shipyard, Pascagoula, 140

IOWA, 83, 86, 115, 147
Isherwood, Benjamin Franklin, 54, 58
Jackson, Harry, 134, 135
Jefferson, Thomas, 8, 9
KANSAS, 91
King Charles II, 1
King Henry VII, 1
King Henry VIII, 2
King, Merrill J., 135
LEADER, 155
League Island, 59, 60, 74, 75, 76, 77, 78, 80, 81, 82, 101
LEXINGTON, 109, 110
Long Beach Navy Yard, 113, 127, 170
LOS ALAMOS, 138, 139
LOUISANA, 91
MAINE, 72, 91
Mallory, Stephen R., 56
Manila Bay, 85, 118
Mare Island floating dry dock, 40, 41
Mare Island Navy Yard, 36, 38, 42, 44, 60, 61, 90
MARY ROSE, 2
MARYLAND, 104
MASSACHUSETTS, 103
McAlpine, William J., 28, 30
McBride, L.B., 91
McCauley, Charles S., 53, 54, 55
MERRIMACK, 53, 54, 55, 56, 57, 125
MICHIGAN, 93
MINNESOTA, 91
MISSISSIPPI, 98
MISSOURI, 91, 127, 128, 129, 147
MONITOR, 54, 56
Monroe, James, 12, 13
MONTANA, 115
Moreel, Ben, 129
NEVADA, 96, 98, 99, 119
NEW JERSEY, 147
NEW MEXICO, 98, 135
NEW YORK, 11, 73, 96, 124
New York Navy Yard, 11, 25, 26, 27, 31, 32, 33, 50, 71, 73, 74, 113, 115, 116, 129
Newport News Shipbuilding and Dry Dock Company, 68, 110, 111

Norfolk Navy Yard, 20, 49, 58, 59, 60, 66, 67, 68, 69, 93, 95, 96, 97, 98, 99, 109, 114, 127
NORTH CAROLINA, 113
Northrop Grumman Newport News, 69, 110, 168
OHIO, 91
OKLAHOMA, 96
Olongapo, 85, 87, 88, 117, 118
OSPREY, 156, 157, 158
Panama Canal, 72, 84, 95, 156, 158
PANAMAX, 168
Paulding, CAPT, 55
Pearl Harbor Navy Yard, 100, 119, 121, 121, 122, 125, 125, 126
PENNSYLVANIA, 25, 32, 53, 54, 96, 120, 134
PHILADELPHIA, 7
Philadelphia Navy Yard, 25, 59, 60, 78, 101, 102, 105, 127
Philadelphia Sectional Dry Dock, 46
PORTSMOUTH, 43, 44,
Portsmouth Navy Yard, 11, 35, 36, 60, 73, 83, 116
POTOMAC, 12, 87
Puget Sound Navy Yard, 83, 93, 113, 114
pumping chamber, 96
PURITAN, 69
Quadrennial Defense Review, 163
Quasi War, 8
RAMSEY, 147
RANGER, 110, 112
Richards, David Kanakeawe, 94
Rodgers, Commodore John, 12, 13
Royal Navy, 1, 2, 3
SARATOGA, 109, 110
Scheib, Captain Tim, 22, 23
SEA SWAN, 156
SHAW, 119, 120
side block, 37, 41, 77, 78, 78, 79, 99, 104, 138, 150, 152, 153
Simpson Dry Dock, 68
sluice gate, 95, 96, 97
South Boston Annex, Boston Navy Yard, 103
SOUTH CAROLINA, 106
SOUTH DAKOTA, 92, 135
Spottswood, Lieutenant C. F. M., 56
Sprowle, Andrew, 3, 8
SPRUANCE, 140, 141
ST MARY'S, 43

ST. LAWRENCE, 32
Stark, Harold R., 112, 115
STEWART, 124
Stuart, Charles B., 27, 33, 36, 48
SUPER SERVANT 3, 155, 156
SYNCROLIFT©, 149, 150, 151, 152, 153, 154
TENNESSEE, 91
Terminal Island, 112, 113, 128
TEXAS, 96
timber dry dock, 60
TITAN, 156
Tracy, Benjamin F., 71
tremie method, 116, 117, 126
Trident Submarine Refit Facilities, 145
UNITED STATES, 6
VERMONT, 91
VICTORY, 2
VIRGINIA, CSS, 54, 55, 57
wale shore, 22, 74, 87
War of 1812, 11, 14
WARREN, 42, 43
WASHINGTON, 11, 91
Washington Navy Yard, 8, 11, 12, 13, 14, 161
Washington, George, 4, 5, 148
WASP, 110
Welles, Gideon, 54
Wilson, Theodore D., 39
WISCONSIN, 98, 99
WYOMING, 96
YANTIC, 68
YFD, 85, 86, 87, 124, 134, 162
YORKTOWN, 110, 111, 125